Advance Praise

"I know Kathy Forti. She was part of my original studies of near-death experiencers, her first episode occurring in 1971. The 'future memory' sequences that so puzzled her then, set the stage for an in-depth study I launched—about aftereffects, about time and space, about science and spirit and soul—which became the unique labyrinth, called *Future Memory*. I promoted her children's books about a boy who had a near-death experience, and for years, as nothing else like it existed at the time. Kathy in many ways was typical of near-death experiencers afterwards—smarter than before, possessed of enhanced faculties, spiritual guidance, younger looking, energetic. Years later she died again.

"Her second near-death experience was intensely powerful, deeper than the previous one, more involved. She returned to life this time so obsessed with numbers and energy signatures and math and science, that it was as if nothing else mattered. Her guidance is continuous, as is her need to understand that guidance. I know this version of Kathy Forti even better than the first, for she found herself poking around into psychotronics, sacred geometry, healing codes, and mind over matter, learning about the people in the past who had proven that spiritual realities were tangible and could transform the world. I know this because this is where my own near-death experiences led me.

"I can personally vouch for what Kathy has discovered and what she has done about this discovery, and the integrity she brings to everything she does. What is so important about what

she later invented—Trinfinity8—is that the device empowers others to develop deeper modes of spirituality as they seek to be of service in the true art of health and healing. *Fractals of God* is a treasure story, not just about what happened to Kathy…but what she found waiting for her…inside her own soul."
-- P.M.H. Atwater, L.H.D. author of *Near-Death Experiences: The Rest of The Story, Future Memory, Children of the Fifth World,* and *We Live Forever*

"Dr. Forti gives us an illuminating peek behind the scenes of her personal life story, spiritual evolution, and metaphysical journey towards the development of the Trinfinity8 technology, a tool for spiritual ascension that affects each person uniquely on their individual path to spiritual evolution. This book is a must for anyone who desires an inspirational read about how to overcome obstacles, see the bigger picture, and learn how to trust in their own inner wisdom against a multitude of odds. *Fractals of God* is an incredible adventure which goes deeply into Kathy's journey of contact with multidimensional beings who desire to assist the human race, to lift the veil of human suffering. She explains in simple terms the codes and algorithms ultimately involved in healing on all levels. All in all, this book is a fascinating read that keeps you eagerly turning the pages to learn more."
-- Tracy Latz, M.D. & Marion Ross, Ph.D. (The Shift Doctors) authors of *Shift: 12 Keys to Shift Your Life* and *Shift: A Woman's Guide to Transformation*

FRACTALS OF GOD

A Psychologist's Near-Death Experience and
Journeys into the Mystical

Kathy J. Forti, Ph.D.

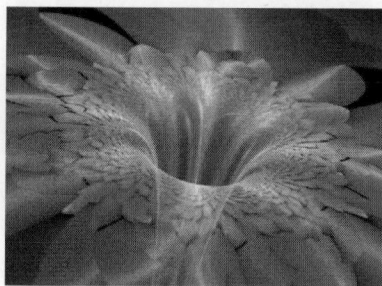

RINNOVO PRESS | May 2014

Cover Art by Gea Annunziata Austen
Book Cover Design by Tracy Andersen

Published and distributed in the United States by Rinnovo Press, May 2014. Books may be ordered through booksellers or by contacting:

Rinnovo Press
1158 – 26th Street, #486
Santa Monica, CA 90403
USA
www.RinnovoPress.com
1-(888)-546-9597

The views expressed in this work are solely those of the author and do not necessarily reflect the views of the publisher, and the publisher hereby disclaims any responsibility for them.

The author of this book does not dispense medical advice or prescribe the use of any technique as a form of treatment for physical, emotional, or medical problems without the advice of a physician, either directly or indirectly. The intent of the author is only to offer information of a general nature to help you in your quest for emotional and spiritual well-being. In the event you use any of the information in this book for yourself, which is your constitutional right, the author and the publisher assume no responsibility for your actions

ISBN 978-0-578-13772-8

Printed in the United States of America

Dedication

For Mom and Dad. I can never thank you enough.
Your love and support gave me the courage
to take risks and soar.

Prologue

"Ask and you shall receive." I'd heard it said at least a hundred times and it had always seemed so naively simplistic to me.

In the course of our lives, we hope and pray for a lot of things to materialize only to have disappointment immediately set in when things don't work out as planned. But appearances can be deceiving. Sometimes, it takes a while to realize on a conscious level that we don't always know what's best for us. Prayers are answered in the most unusual ways. Even our failures turn out to be blessings in disguise, giving us a whole new and possibly more enlightening perspective and direction. Having trust in the outcome may be the ultimate lesson.

Yet trust was the one ingredient I seemed to lack most back in 1981 when I asked in prayers that I be allowed to be of real service to those who most needed it. It was a responsibility I thought I'd be ready to act on—no questions asked. No sooner had I pledged it than I found myself put to the test.

At the time, I was working with children at New York City's Ronald McDonald House, "a home-away-from-home" for children treated for cancer at nearby hospitals like Memorial Sloan Kettering. I was the assistant manager, helping run the House, and I loved working there. Months earlier, I had quit my job at WCBS-TV New York's "Eye On New York"—a magazine-style format show where I worked my way up from researcher to field producer right after graduating from New York University's School of Broadcast Journalism. One of my last jobs as a field producer was working on a story about the newly opened New York City Ronald McDonald House. The day I walked in the House, I had this over-powering feeling that I belonged there amidst those brave souls facing everyday life-and-death situations. As a result, I started volunteering my free time on evenings and some weekends when I could break away from my production duties at WCBS-TV. It wasn't long before one of the Ronald McDonald House's Board Members offered me a job helping run the House as assistant house manager. I took it without hesitation. I quit the news business and, instead, did a 180-degree turn right into the healthcare field working a job that was less than half my former pay. My friends thought I was crazy, and I couldn't fault them for it. I felt a strong calling to make the change, and so I went with it. At the time I would have been loath to explain why—it just felt right.

Helping manage the day-to-day running of the house and meeting families going through the most challenging time of their lives was a real eye-opener for me. It put what was important in life into clearer perspective. For the first time, I felt a sense of real fulfillment. It was like working in a little United Nations, a house where both children and parents from all corners of the world came to stay, seeking hope and a cure. It was where I first met Fernanda.

There were so many children I'd come to know there—all beautiful in their own special way. But from the minute I first saw Fernanda, there was something about her which instantly drew me. I simply could not take my eyes off her. She was nine years old, blond-haired, with cherub blue eyes and a radiant smile that made you want to just rush up and put your arms around her. She looked like a little angel and could light up a room. Both she and her mother had come all the way from Sao Paulo, Brazil, hoping to find a cure for Fernanda's advancing leukemia.

From the start, our friendship was to be a limited one, simply because I didn't speak her native Portuguese, and Fernanda spoke no English. I found I could muddle through a few words I picked up here and there, but basically I had to rely on her mother to translate everything for me. And then, not more than a week after they arrived, they were gone as quickly as they'd come—checked out, leaving not a word behind. I presumed the medical prognosis had not been good, and they'd decided to return to their native land. It happened often. Another face in passing, another sad story. I soon forgot about Fernanda until one night, a month later, when we met again—only this time in a dream.

It was not an earth-shattering dream by any means; actually it was quite short and simple. But it was one I was not likely to forget, for its vividness was stunningly real. It was a dream which brought me to a certain hospital room, where Fernanda lay in a bed sleeping quite soundly. She wore emerald green pajamas. As I looked down on her, I heard a man's voice behind me say, "Go to her. You have a message for her." I never saw the man's face, much as I would have liked to. Yet, it was his words that were more important. I sensed a real urgency behind them. I remember being confused and immediately blurted out, "But I don't speak her language."

The voice, with ever so much patience, calmly responded, "That's not important. You have a message for her and need to go see her." Before I could voice any further objections or doubts about being able to deliver this mysterious "message," I was jarred awake by the sound of my alarm clock going off, and the urgency that if I didn't get moving I'd miss my train into the city. Yet I couldn't stop wondering at the dream's meaning, and the thought of it continued to nag at me all morning, like an obsession. Was it possible, I wondered, that Fernanda was still in New York after all and hadn't returned to Brazil? I knew if I was to have any peace of mind, there was only one way to find out. I dialed Memorial Sloan Kettering Hospital, where she had initially sought treatment, to see what I could find out. Five minutes later, I learned all I needed to know. Fernanda had undergone a bone marrow transplant at the hospital two days earlier—a procedure that at the time had a very low success rate. I hung up the phone wondering what to do next, even as I realized I already knew. For some unfathomable reason, I had to go see her.

I skipped lunch, worrying every step of the way to the hospital. In my mind I kept going over and over again what this message I had to give her could possibly be. Was she perhaps dying and I was expected to give her or her family some words of comfort? I felt a nervous sweat steal over me brought on by the same kind of stage fright an actor experiences just before he goes on and suddenly realizes in panic that he can't remember a single line. At worst, I feared I'd been sent on a mission I'd probably screw up and no one "up there" would ever call on me to be of service ever again. It was a depressing thought. "Well what did you expect?!" I wanted to shout back. "I've gotten zero briefing on what to say!"

I stalled in the hospital's gift shop, picking out a fuzzy teddy bear, trying to ward off the negative energy I always feel when I step into a hospital or medical institution. It's not just from the sick people staying there. The Ronald McDonald House was full of sick kids, yet the energy there was full of love, hope, sharing, and the promise of a brighter tomorrow. Attitude, I had learned, can make a huge difference. And right then and there I suddenly realized that my own attitude needed some adjustment. I had to stop worrying about what I was supposed to do and just trust in the belief that somehow, at the right moment in time, I'd do it.

With the teddy bear clutched to my chest like some misplaced adult security blanket, I made my way to the pediatric oncology unit, stopping just outside Fernanda's room where a sign informed me she had been placed in "reverse isolation." She literally had no immunity to fight off even the simplest cold germs from me or anyone else. Slowly, I donned the sterile white gown, mask, gloves and booties set out for visitors, took a deep breath, and softly knocked on the door.

Her mother cracked the door open a few inches, then opened it wide as recognition and surprise registered at once on her tired face. "Please come in," she beckoned in a whisper.

I slipped quietly inside and saw Fernanda lying in the bed curled up under the covers. And just like I had seen in my dream, she was wearing those emerald green pajamas. That certainly got my attention.

Taking an empty seat beside her mother, I asked her to bring me up to date. Fernanda's mother needed to talk, so I just listened. Upon learning that Fernanda needed an operation and extended treatment, they left the Ronald McDonald House to rent an apartment closer to the hospital. Fernanda's younger brother had been tested back in Brazil, and the entire family was relieved to learn he was a perfect match as a bone marrow donor. Within days of learning this news, both the father and son flew to New York to prepare for the procedure. Alone in their small apartment, they felt isolated in such a big city. It was clear that the uncertain waiting was taking its toll on the entire family. Suddenly, Fernanda's mother paused and looked at me curiously. "What brought you here today to visit?" she asked.

Even though I had expected that very question, it still unnerved me that I had to answer it. I quickly debated how crazy it would sound to tell her the truth. But, I decided to chance it. I told her about the dream and this strange, but strong, need to visit. I conveniently left out the part that I had a message for them. As I spoke, I had the odd feeling that I delivered the dream into her hands and it was now up to her to make some sense of it. I sincerely hoped that whatever the message was, it would somehow unfold on its own.

As I finished my brief explanation, she got up and went directly to the telephone without saying another word. I could see her finger trembling as she dialed a familiar number. She spoke, and as it connected to the person she was trying to reach, a torrent of Portuguese spilled forth. I could barely hear the excited response from the person she was talking with. It was terrible not being able to understand a word. I could only sit there dumbfounded as tears suddenly streamed uncontrollably from the woman's eyes, her voice rising and falling with emotion. I felt a rising sense of panic at not understanding what was taking place.

"Is everything alright? Please tell me," I finally asked.

It was as though she had forgotten me until my voice reminded her that I was still there, waiting. A few seconds later, she hung up. When she turned to me, I could see tears of joy in her eyes. She bridged the distance and embraced me, relief evident in every fiber of her body. It felt like her whole heart and soul reached out, not wanting to let go, as if needing to confirm that I was indeed real. I felt emotionally overwhelmed as well. I started crying with her, even though I was still clueless as to why.

"That was my husband," she explained, choking back tears. "He's been praying to God every day that Fernanda will come through the transplant—we both have. But the other day, he asked for a sign from heaven that Fernanda would live. Since we know no one in your country, he asked that the sign be an *unexpected visitor.* You have answered that prayer."

I sat back down again, feeling not only a sense of awe but total incredulity. Not for one second had it mattered that I speak her language. The language had been a silent one. I had only to be there at that point in time. My presence was the message.

For days afterward, I marveled at the variables that had to be programmed into some cosmic computer to make all the right connections possible. I felt humbled at being allowed the privilege of delivering such a message—along with the sense of completion of bringing joy and hope into someone else's life when it was so desperately needed.

Fernanda eventually returned to Brazil with her family and the life ahead that was promised her. She recovered, and, last I heard (which was many years ago), was doing very well. Yet, looking at the bigger picture, Fernanda's father was not the only one that had received a confirmation sign. I had been going through my own life changes at the time and, prior to this dream, had asked for a specific sign that I was on the right track. I received my sign and, in turn, I had to be someone else's sign—Fernanda's. Either way, it was a true lesson in trusting one's own inner guidance—a theme that would continually come up throughout my life.

The message for Fernanda was just my initial dress rehearsal for the bigger assignment I would be given later in life. When you make a covenant with God to be of service, sooner or later that call will be answered.

Table of Contents

Chapter 1
AN AWAKENING

"Death is no more than passing from one room to another. But there's a difference for me, you know. Because in that other room I shall be able to see." – HELEN KELLER

Any event, whether large or small, can shift your whole world where nothing is ever the same again. It can happen several times in a lifetime, necessitating making small adjustments along our life's path – our spiritual journey. I'd come to recognize that when I resisted something, it usually persisted until I self-corrected and made a better choice. When things go wrong, it seems to be the universe's way of saying, "Kathy, you are off your path. Now get back on and things will start falling into place again." So by 2003, with a lot more hits and misses under my belt, I felt I had gained a little bit more wisdom in navigating my life path—or so I thought.

On the evening of May 15, 2003, my life path opened onto a cosmic avenue. I had come a long way since my journalism news and Ronald McDonald House days back in the '70s. I was now a clinical psychologist in private practice in Los Angeles, and was finishing up seeing clients for the day. My last client, a devout Buddhist, informed me before leaving that this evening was the beginning of a "Wesak Full Moon Lunar Eclipse" which just so happened to coincide with one of the high holy days for Buddhists. She told me tonight's moon was a special alignment that created a bridge between Heaven and Earth, and she and many others would be in meditation that evening. I remember her telling me that this event was looked upon as a unique opportunity to assist in expanding the consciousness of humanity. I smiled and said good-bye. To me it was just another night; I was tired and ready to go home.

As I walked to my car, parked in an open lot adjacent to my office building, I glanced up at the moon. It looked like the moon on any other night, not necessarily any brighter or dimmer. Unlike my client, it held no real significance for me. My mind was too busy going over my current clinical caseload. I had a number of very challenging clients, and I wondered if anything I was doing was really making a difference. Every therapist questions their effectiveness at some time or another—some more so than others. Since the attack on the World Trade Center, it felt like the clients I saw were even more fear-based and anxiety-ridden than ever before. You could clearly divide life into pre-9/11 and post-9/11 thinking. The world had clearly changed and my job, like many other mental health professionals, had become more difficult. Was I ready for a change? Sure, but I had no idea what direction or form it might take.

Just as I was reaching for my car door handle, I felt an unusual "whoosh" move out of my chest area. It was so dramatic and unexpected that it stopped me in my tracks, making me wonder-- "what the hell was that?" It felt like something had left my physical body, and I was now no longer the same person I was seconds earlier. I felt totally bereft. I felt a profound sense of emptiness, a sense of acute loss like nothing I had ever experienced. It felt akin to what one might feel if they had suddenly lost their entire family. And with it came the startlingly clear knowledge that I was done with my work here on Earth, as I knew it. All this happened within seconds. Feelings and thoughts, which were foreign to me, now took center stage. I had no idea what had just happened.

I didn't consider medical assistance as I didn't feel sick, nor was I suffering any pain. My breathing appeared normal and my motor function was certainly capable of driving myself home without incident. It was just a weird and strange experience, and I didn't know what to make of it. Being a psychologist, I naturally went into my over-analytical drive. I made myself some soothing hot tea when I got home and propped myself up against the bed pillows. The warmth of the tea did nothing to dispel the feeling I still had that I was "done with my work as I knew it."

I started to examine my life, looking for clues that might explain this pervasive feeling. Could I be secretly depressed and not be in touch with my true feelings? I didn't think so. My health was good; I wasn't rich but my practice was doing well enough to pay my bills. I divorced years earlier, but that split was amicable, and there was currently no love interest in my life or relationship complications. My family was close emotionally, but not geographically. My sister and her husband lived in New York, my brother in Florida, and my parents still lived in our childhood home in Chicago. Although my parents were aging and in their 80's, they were still fairly self-sufficient and mobile. So, nothing I could think of explained where my thoughts were presently focused.

It occurred to me that perhaps this feeling that my "work was done here on Earth as I knew it" was because I was getting ready to die. Quickly following that thought was an even worse one: "What if I'm not getting ready to die and I have to feel this way for the rest of my life?" If I lived another 20, 30, or 40 years feeling this sense of total emptiness, then I knew it was going to suck big time. My life had always been purpose-driven. I couldn't fathom the thought of feeling empty and finished. I suddenly could not think of a future goal I had at that moment except to make sense of what was currently happening to me.

And that's when my life shifted. One second, I was totally conscious sipping my tea; the next minute, the edges of my vision went into a soft blurry focus and all I could see was an old wooden radio receiver with knobs, atop a pedestal, under an open canopied tent in the middle of a vast green field. As I moved towards the radio without conscious physical effort, I saw a swirling spiral vortex in my head moving faster and faster as I was sucked into the radio. I felt myself shoot through the center of the vortex pattern into a large dark tunnel—horizontal, feet first. I no longer felt I was in my physical body, but I was still aware of its form. It felt incredibly light. I was aware that I was moving through this tunnel at a high rate of speed. It felt very familiar. I knew I had been there before. Even though I was travelling horizontal, I could see light at the end of the tunnel—a brilliant light that pulsed and glowed. That's when it hit me. "Oh my God—this is THAT tunnel!" A rush of thoughts immediately bombarded me. "Did I just die? What did I die from? I wasn't sick. What happened? Is this it?!" I felt in full command of my faculties and they were processing this infor-mation at warp speed.

Oddly enough, I didn't feel anxious or scared. A sense of acceptance and amazement quickly took hold. I was on my way to The LIGHT—wow. There was the briefest of seconds when I thought: "Oh. My life is over. How quick was that?!" But it was immediately replaced with intense curiosity. I figured if I had indeed died, there wasn't much I could do about it now, so I should just go with it. Better to not fight the process and see where it took me. This would be MY great adventure. Looking back, it's amazing what goes through your head during such times. I recall having the fleeting thought that perhaps I should be flying through this tunnel like Superman instead of horizontal, feet first, like I was on some invisible conveyor belt. Yet, somehow I knew this was my method of transportation. We all do it differently. I knew without knowing why, that this was how I always did it. I just knew it was faster.

Unlike other near-death experiences, I was not aware of angelic beings or departed love ones in the tunnel. There was no celestial music, psychedelic colors or light beings coming to greet me. I had no life review. I had the distinct feeling, more than once, that I had done this before and no longer needed the welcoming band. I was alone and my consciousness was very focused. I had a clear, all-knowing feeling that the tunnel I was in was an energy conversion device that allowed one's energy to be sped up or slow down depending on the density of the plane you were departing and/or entering. I knew the Earth plane was a lot heavier and denser than where I was going. The tunnel was helping me synchronize my energy body.

I was aware that my body was being prepped as I moved faster towards the White Light. It felt beckoning and familiar. It felt like I was going home and all would be well. I recalled briefly thinking of my family and knew they would grieve, but would ultimately be okay. I didn't feel any true regrets. I didn't have a husband or children back home who would be devastated by my unexpected departure. Nothing held me back. I was excited to be where I was going. I felt liberated. Then, right before I could move into the Light, I stopped—or rather it felt like something stopped me. I just hovered at the edge of the Light. I could feel it beckoning me, but I was unable to move forward into it. I say that because I consciously tried to will myself forward, thinking I should have that ability and power now. I tried several times, without success. I never heard of anyone being stuck in the tunnel. Perhaps this is what they meant by being stuck in limbo? I waited thinking if I let go of my expectations, I could slide right into the Light—perhaps it was a test. I don't know how long I was hovering there waiting for something to happen when I had the irreverent thought, "Well, this is boring!"

With that thought, there was an implosion of energy coming from the Light, which directly infused into me. I felt it in every cell of my being. It pulsed with life and felt expansive, ancient and wise. As it streamed into me, I spun back around with great intentional force and was propelled back through the tunnel as fast as could be--again, horizontal, feet first. There seemed to be some urgency in my being sent back at such a rapid speed.

I heard encouraging voices in my head saying: "Breathe, Kathy, breathe." I had no clue to the identity of these voices or how much time had passed, but their words were somehow comforting. With a jolt, I suddenly found myself slammed back into my physical body, only to discover my whole left side was completely paralyzed and the rest of me felt very weak. I couldn't move, and I was alone without help. There's that brief moment of panic when you realize you can't reach a phone, no one is there, and how helpless and vulnerable you truly are. The voices in my head continued to soothe me, telling me to breathe easy, relax and all would be well. I have no way of medically proving this, but I know with all certainty that my heart had somehow stopped and they (whoever they were) were trying to get me to breathe life back into my physical form. From a psychological standpoint, hearing voices in your head is not the most comforting thought. I certainly had treated patients who fell into that diagnostic category. So it was only natural I had a moment, or perhaps more than a moment, of questioning my sanity.

However, I quickly realized there wasn't any other choice but to listen to the voices and accept their helpful instruction. As I lay there unable to move, I was very much aware of my body being worked on and being re-connected by some unseen source. I could hear clicks in my head as parts of my body came back on-line and feeling slowly returned. I felt tremendous relief and gratitude. My body was working again. Underneath me, I realized the mattress was wet. The tea I had been sipping prior to my tunnel experience had spilled all over the bedding.

I attempted to move from the bed, but noticed there was still a little pressure in my heart area. It concerned me. I worried that I would have to see a cardiologist as soon as possible to make sure I hadn't done some kind of irreparable damage to my heart. The voices returned to tell me that seeing a doctor was not necessary--I would be all right. They knew what they were doing, for within hours after my experience, the pressure subsided in my chest area and I was filled with new energy.

When I say "new energy," I mean like after you've had a blood transfusion and feel ready to run a marathon. I no longer felt empty, but enormously full. I knew I wasn't getting ready to die, because I was pretty sure I had almost done that already, and God wasn't yet ready to allow me to make that final leap. I had the feeling that if I had made that leap, I would not have wanted to come back. And I was pretty sure that there must be a very good reason for all that had happened, and why I returned. I didn't yet consciously know what it was, but I was soon to find out.

Chapter 2
GEEKDOM

"Choice, not chance, determines your destiny." - *ARISTOTLE*

Within 24 hours after returning to my physical body, an unusual shift began to take place. My mind and thoughts were filled with the world of science and physics, and more specifically-- quantum physics and mathematics. I had not entertained much of a passing interest in any of these areas prior to my experience, but now it bordered on obsessive thinking, like a junkie needing a fix.

I'd go to bed and like clockwork I would wake up between 3:00 and 4:00 a.m. every night with scientific queries running through my head. Thoughts about dimensional planes, torques, energy, and most of all math, overwhelmed me. I literally could not return to sleep unless I physically got myself out of bed and went to my computer to research each and every string of thought—including String Theory. It opened a whole new world to me. Nights became my special classes. Every evening, I felt like I was getting up to speed in understanding more than just Physics 101. What truly amazed me was I actually understood what I read. Somehow, as a result of my experience, I unlocked a part of my brain where higher concepts and a love of science and mathematics resided.

I was fascinated to learn all about such visionary inventors such as Nikola Tesla, who had not only invented Alternating

Current (AC), which we use today (most people erroneously think Thomas Edison discovered it), but that he also found the solution to abundant world-wide free energy. This discovery was buried when the financial banker J. P Morgan, who helped initially fund Tesla's research, pulled all funding after realizing he could not make money from free energy.

I wondered why I had not heard about Tesla from science books in school. Just about every engineer and physicist knows about his inventions. Back in the early 1900's, he had already foreseen that the world would be wireless one day and proposed how to do it. Marconi stole Tesla's ideas and got credit for the radio. Today, Tesla has hundreds of US patents that are hidden under lock and key under the protection of national security by the U.S. Department of Defense. Tesla's inventions, which included levitation and the teleportation of objects and quite possibly man, could and most likely would change our world.

My nighttime schooling became even more interesting when I heard those same familiar voices in my head make comments about the information I read on the Internet. I noticed that I was steered away from some website research which they appeared to think had little or no merit—mainly no scintilla of "Truth." They (the voices) were big on Truth. When I first read something about the Hadron Super Collider in Cern, Switzerland, and their search for the "God Particle" or the "Higgs boson," which is a hypothetical particle that physicists believe gives all other particles mass and therefore explains our origins, they said the information was not accurate, but it was as far as we as a race had gotten in our knowledge of the universe. I was told there is no definitive or finite God particle. Even in what looks like a finite structure, there is still infiniteness. The universe is a hologram with universes within universes. There is no beginning, nor end, but a continuous circuitous loop—almost toroidal in shape. I took this to mean that, no matter how many times they broke apart a particle, they would still find another even smaller particle--much like those Russian Matryoshka dolls. A doll, within a doll, within a doll to infinity.

Night after night, I spent hours in front of the computer learning about the world of energy, and then saw clients the next day without feeling the least bit tired. The information fed me. It's not like I would ever be competent to teach it, but, more important, I felt compelled to understand what was infinitely possible in our world and quite possibly worlds beyond. There was a vast Source of information out there, and it was helping me to expand my world.

I was hesitant at first to tell anyone what had happened to me as a result of my tunnel or, more accurately, what I was certain was a near-death experience (NDE). Had I told my family, they would worry that there was something wrong with me—either emotionally or physically-- and I didn't want to have to deal with that. I wanted to keep it to myself for a while—to be free to ponder its implications without having it be contaminated by others people's thoughts or concerns for my welfare.

Returning to work now seemed different. At first, I thought it was my imagination, but I began to notice a side effect from my NDE experience. I now felt my client's emotional states and had become much more sensitive to the world around me, which did not feel good. Picking up people's thoughts might sound like a handy ability to have as a therapist, but when you feel other people's anger and don't know where it's coming from at first, it can definitely have a negative effect on you.

I decided it was time to bring in an expert opinion—someone I already knew and had successfully worked with in the past. E. M. "Gene" Nicolay, who co-wrote *The System Lords and the Twelve Dimensions,* is a rare anomaly. He was born with the gift to see beyond the veil, to look into a soul's history, and the ability to predict future events. He was always incredibly accurate, and, to this day, I recall events he predicted years ago which are even now occurring. I had worked with Gene on very difficult cases in the past where clients were clearly stuck, and, with their permission, he would look behind the scenes from a soul level, report why things were happening, and help them more easily navigate the problem. He never wanted to know anything about the client. He only needed their name—making for a clean read without background information to color his thinking. He had been a Godsend of insight for a number of psychologists over the years. I respected his methods and expertise, and so I called him and, without telling him what I had experienced, I asked him to take a look behind the scenes and see what was going on with me.

He took what seemed like forever, when perhaps it was only no more than a few minutes, when he suddenly said: "Well, Kathy--you almost died. But the weird thing is that all your old Guides have left."

I recalled that "whoosh" feeling that had come from my chest area when I walked to my parked car—followed immediately by the feeling like I had lost something very dear and familiar to me. At the time, I had no idea what that meant. That was my Guides leaving? Plural?? I believed in spirit guides, or what some people might refer to as guardian angels, but nowhere had I ever read of guidance leaving and feeling such a profound sense of loneliness as a result.

"Yes," he confirmed, already answering my unspoken thoughts. "Your old Guides left to make room for a new set of guidance. These new Guides are very technologically oriented. More specialized—kind of geeky."

I recalled that incredible influx of energy I received in the tunnel. It had infused my entire cellular being and almost immediately afterward, I began hearing those helpful voices. I had new Guides. No wonder I had felt like someone or something was trying to get me up to speed each night with my obsessive Internet Physics 101 lessons. The first words out of my mouth were: "What do they want?"

Gene was already a step ahead of me. "They're telling me it was a pre-contract you made prior to coming into this life." He hesitated, grasping for words. "They're showing me that you came back to invent some type of electronic device."

"What?" I said in disbelief.

"They're saying that it's some kind of medical device that will change people's concept about healing. It's rather complicated to explain."

This sounded preposterous to me. I was a therapist, not an inventor. "I don't know anything about electronics or inventing medical devices," I protested.

He hesitated. "Well, they're saying they will help you and point you to the right people who will be instrumental in helping you. They seem quite certain about it."

I thought perhaps they had gotten the wrong girl—mixed me up with someone else who would better fit the bill. "I don't think so," I said, while silently wondering if Gene was slipping in his ability to read the other side. Up until now, his batting average for accuracy had been extremely good. There was no way this news fit in with where I saw my life going—or rather where I thought it was supposed to go.

"Whatever it is you agreed to do, they're saying it will change the way people think about healing," he added.

I remained silent. It was like he could hear me frowning on the other end of the phone, resistant to whatever other bombshells he might be ready to drop.

"I'm just the messenger," he said. I'd been on the other end of being someone's messenger, so I just shut up and told him I would think about it. And despite not trying to think about it—it soon became an obsession.

I wasn't a stranger to unusual experiences over the years. When I was very young, I would sometimes tell people my name wasn't really Kathy. Every time I heard the song "They Call the Wind Mariah," I would correct it and say, "No. They call me Zaria." My mother would call me her "little actress" and, thinking I was either creating a character for myself, or worse yet lying, she would just shake her head. I wasn't sure if her reaction was one of resigned tolerance or displeasure, but not wanting to displease her, I learned to keep what I thought was my real name to myself.

However, I knew from this early age on that there was something significant I needed to do with my life. Maybe it wouldn't be important to anyone else, but it felt important to me. I remember knowing before I was a teenager that I would not have children or the traditional married family life most women long for and experience. I also knew it was very unusual not to have these desires and even odder that I seemed perfectly okay with this. I had no idea what it was I was supposed to do when I grew up. I entertained the thought that perhaps I would be a nurse and help others heal. As those years passed, my life took shape and form, and I went into the psychotherapy field, I thought the important thing I felt driven to do was probably to just be the best therapist I could be. But life oftentimes has other plans.

Kathy J. Forti, Ph.D.

Chapter 3
MYSTICAL BEGINNINGS

"We are a way for the cosmos to know itself."
– CARL SAGAN

My first profound mystical experience happened when I was 18 years old. Something opened for me and allowed me a glimpse into the beyond before I was even consciously aware of the possibilities. At the time, I was a student at the University of Chicago, while also attending the Art Institute's School of the Goodman Theatre in Chicago, where I grew up. That little actress my mother first saw in me was encouraged to blossom and grow. She enrolled me in children's theatre and drama classes from the time I was 10 years old. I did community theatre and enjoyed it. I wasn't a great singer or dancer and was a mediocre actress at best, but my mother loved the theatre, and I think a part of me was trying to live her unfulfilled dream. So there I was, enrolled in the School of the Goodman Theatre, trying to make it in the acting field. As a freshman, I was assigned to the stage crew on the Berthold Brecht play *Baal* about a wastrel youth who becomes involved in several sexual affairs and a murder.

It was late when I finished putting away stage props and costumes—well after midnight. Back in October 1971, Chicago's Grant Park parking lot was open air and adjacent to the Goodman Theatre, and I was walking to my parked car to go home. (As I write this, I suddenly realize there seems to be a pattern or theme with me regarding walking to my car and strange events occurring. I'm not sure why it never occurred to me before.)

I was in another world, tired, thinking about the day, and not paying attention to the fact that the large expanse of parking lot was fairly deserted, and I was a woman alone. You don't think about these things when you're young, and you think nothing bad can happen to you—only to other people. Too late, I heard footsteps behind me coming closer as I approached my car. I turned just as an African American male in his late 20's was upon me with a knife. He pushed me against my driver side door, pressed a knife to my throat, and told me to get in the car or he would hurt me. I realized all too late that I was in a deserted corner of the parking lot, where no one would hear me yelling for help, even if I could open my mouth to scream.

He took my keys from my hand and pushed me inside the back seat. As he wielded the knife and told me to do what he said, I thought I was going to die. I could picture myself dead in a coffin with my parents grieving, and I deeply regretted never being able to say goodbye. The thought of never seeing them again was devastating. With such anguish, a swelling panic rose in my throat and I wanted to start sobbing hysterically. I was sure this was going to be the way I died -- raped and killed before I even got my life off to a running start.

As that hysteria rose within me, my focus blurred, and I suddenly saw a huge movie screen open in my mind's eye. I saw flashes of a brief life review, like snapshots of the greatest hits in event format meshed with feelings and emotions. There wasn't much there. I was only 18, but then it was like I jumped forward and saw myself as a much older woman. I was sitting in a living room in a black lacquered Chinese rocking chair and two faceless children were sitting at my feet. I was reading to them from a children's book. I could clearly see the soft green paint of the room's wall, the rounded arched entryway, and a beautiful wooden antique hutch with white ironstone glassware displayed on its shelves. It was so crystal clear that this was me in the future, and that I was going to survive to be an older woman. I was not going to die. During the seconds it took me to have this all-knowing experience and realize my fate, the panic in me immediately dissipated. An incredible calm came over me as the movie screen disappeared. To this day, I am certain that vision saved me. Had I not seen it, I would have become hysterical and my attacker would have used the knife to shut me up—and I probably would have died. Some divine intelligence wanted me to know I would survive and be okay, if only I didn't do something stupid like over-react.

As a result, I was able to detach myself from the actual rape, seeing myself watching from above my body, not understanding how that could be at the time, but accepting it. I focused on the bright light of a street lamp I could see through the car's windows. I felt I merged into that light and was only somewhat aware of the pain my body was experiencing from the rape of an 18-year-old virgin. I lived through the experience as the vision had shown me.

Seven years later, I would walk into my boyfriend's (later to become my husband's) home in New York for the first time and revisit that future scene from my pre-rape experience. Just like I had been shown in the vision, there was the arched entry living room with the soft pale green walls and the black Chinese rocking chair—and of course that antique hutch in detail, just like I had seen it. I almost fell to my knees at the shock of seeing this all again.

As a side note to this, I am no longer with that husband. We divorced six years later, and he's now deceased. But that vision of hope allowed me to tap into a *possible future*. I believe we work with possibilities and potentials all the time, but nothing is ever written in stone due to the power of free choice and self-discovery. The two "faceless" children I saw in my rape-saving vision were faceless because I eventually chose not to have children. However, I did choose to write several published children's books that I have read to many a child, just like I saw myself doing in the vision. At the age of 18, I didn't have a clue I might write a children's book someday, but that possible future was already in the ethers waiting for me if I reached for it. So it shouldn't have come as any big surprise to me that my second brush with life and death in 2003 would bring anything less profound.

I was raised in an Italian Catholic neighborhood on the Northwest side of Chicago. My father was Italian, my mother Polish and, at the time, it seemed the only heritage that really mattered was my Sicilian side of the family. We struggled financially as my father tried to build a kitchen and bath remodeling business on less than a high school diploma. His own father had died when he was two years old, and my father had to drop out of school to help support his mother and sister. He had a strong sense of responsibility for his family and worked long hard hours building his business into what would eventually be a financial success. He was a Horatio Alger type of man. A strong determination, coupled with innate drawing and design skills, made him rise to the top even without a formal education. My mother was also a very artistic and creative person, who graduated from junior college. She sang, she drew, she acted—yet she put it aside and helped my father realize his dreams at the expense of her own.

When I think of all the therapy clients I've seen over the years and the horror stories of their childhoods, I consider myself extremely lucky. My parents were always supportive and encouraging to all their children, and they loved us dearly. Had I not had that strong foundation of acceptance and love, I would probably be a totally different person today.

I'm a middle child with a sister two years older and a brother five years younger. I went to St. William's Elementary School right around the block from where we lived, and later the all-girls Catholic high school, Mother Theodore Guerin, in River Grove, Illinois. As a kid, I would do anything to get out of going to church. I didn't see myself as particularly religious and, to be totally honest, I thought most of the nuns that taught me were a little bit strange, to say the least. Even as a kid, I knew some of them seemed almost zealously over-punitive. My piano teacher, Sister Catherine, struck my hands with a ruler if I didn't observe the correct upright form while playing. Because of it, I stopped wanting to learn piano.

I had a sense of wanting to do something meaningful to help others. My early aspirations were to be a nurse, after reading books on the lives of Florence Nightingale and Clara Barton. A therapist was not too far off the mark. And, oddly enough, I became a therapist out of intimidation. My undergraduate bachelor's degree was in broadcast journalism from New York University. When my post-graduate job at WCBS-TV led me to work at the New York City Ronald McDonald House, I found myself working with families facing life and death issues while their children were being treated for cancer. We had a house library full of self-help books for adults, but nothing addressing these issues for children. I decided to write a book about a little boy who has a near-death experience and meets a spiritual guide that help him to learn about his true-life purpose. It came pouring out of me like it was already written. It was called *The Door to the Secret City.* Yes, years earlier the blueprint for my life was already taking shape. Life would eventually imitate fiction. But how this revelation came to be was even stranger, so let me back up a little and tell you the opening that led to it.

I love books. I love to read, and I used to have this fun way of discovering new literature. I would be at a bookstore, close my eyes and let my fingers run along the book spines and see where it stopped when I re-opened my eyes. "Give me something good to read," I would say silently to myself. On one particular day in December of 1980, my fingers stopped on the book *Journeys Out of Body* by Robert Monroe. Up until then I had never heard about an out-of-body experience. It wasn't talked about back in the early 1980s, and I had never seen references to it in movies or TV shows like we so often do today.

I opened the book and started reading. I was fascinated to learn we had astral bodies. I remember flashing back to my rape experience, and how during the attack I oddly saw myself hovering over my body and looking down on the experience. Up until that point, I hadn't thought much about why that was. Reading this book got me to thinking. I sat down on the floor in the middle of the bookstore, totally captivated. Needless to say, I purchased the book, took it home, and devoured it. In the back were exercises to practice attaining an out-of-body experience (OBE).

I've since learned in life that when you have no great expectation for the outcome, amazing things often happen. I call it my neutral-idling state. That night back in 1980, I decided to give it a go and try for an OBE. I didn't expect anything to happen. No one expects things to happen first time out, unless of course you have some kind of beginner's luck. So I lay down in my bed and began the breathing and visualization exercises as instructed. As I started really getting into it, I felt my body sink down into the ticking of the mattress. I felt light and heavy at the same time. And I was suddenly aware that I could no longer feel parts of myself. I was separating from my physical body. Just as I became aware of this, I saw a swirling vortex in my head (somewhat similar to my NDE), followed by a light-headedness. My next thought was "Oh my God, it's really happening!" With that thought, total fear flooded in, and the experience shut down immediately. I was relieved and disappointed at the same time. It had scared the hell out of me.

One part of me kicked myself for ruining what could have been an amazing experience had I not been such a coward. After convincing myself to give it another go, I then tried to make it happen again, and nothing, nada. I'd blown it. No second chances.

That week, I flew home to Chicago to be with my family for the Christmas holidays. One evening we had a group of people over, and in the background, the television was turned on in the living room to some local TV talk show. No one was paying any attention to it. It was background sound; but then something made me glance over, and I saw a familiar face being interviewed by the show's host. It was Caroline Myss (before she wrote all her books). I went to high school with Caroline, and we had been in many of the same classes together. The lower third of the screen identified her as a "Paranormal Psychologist." I moved closer to the TV, and, lo and behold, she was talking about out-of-body experiences! I was glued to the screen. I knew I had to get in touch with her. Did she still live in Chicago, I wondered?

My mother saved everything and, sure enough, I was able to locate my old Mother Theodore Guerin phone directory. I called Caroline's family home, and her mother gave me her current home number. We got together two days later for dinner, and I told her all about my aborted out-of-body attempt.

"You must go to the Monroe Institute in Virginia," she told me. "Bob Monroe does training workshops."

"Oh, my God, I was just reading his book!" I said. How co-incidental was that? I didn't recall there being anything in the book about workshops. The timing with learning this bit of information was more than synchronistic.

Caroline told me she had been there a year earlier when the Institute had first opened, and it was a defining experience for her. She warned me that it was expensive, but definitely worth it. I was so excited, I was literally buzzing.

I called the Institute immediately and got a reservation for May, 1981—enough time to save up some money to pay for a weeklong workshop. I was married at the time, and my husband Steve seemed perplexed with my sudden interest in astral travel. He came from high academia, and I think he thought he was indulging a whim of mine. It would also mean getting time off from my job at the New York City Ronald McDonald House. I was determined to go no matter what.

When May finally came around, it seemed like it had been an eternity of waiting. The Institute was on a small ranch in the foothills of the Blue Ridge Mountains outside Faber, Virginia near Charlottesville. It was a small workshop group of about 20 individuals and what was most unusual was that only three in the group were women. I had never been to a workshop before where males dominated. I didn't know it at the time, but this would make a difference.

I was assigned to share the room with a local girl named Leticia. We each had what they called a "CHEC unit" which resembled an enclosed Pullman berth fitted with a waterbed mattress and sound speakers built into the walls. You crawled into your CHEC unit and it was quite cozy, like a womb. It was in this CHEC unit where we would experience our out-of-body training through the use of frequency sound therapy piped in from the main control room. No subliminal programming was involved, just sound to help induce altered states that could lead to astral travel. It was a big "if," and Bob Monroe told us to forget about any expectations we might have, which is hard to do when you fly long distance and invest a lot of money specifically for the very purpose of being taught how to have an out-of-body experience. Many of us were frustrated trying to make it happen and coming up empty-handed. Bob would instruct us to put our thoughts, worries, and baggage in some kind of visualized "energy conversion box" of our own making prior to embarking on each training tape. In this conversion box, we tried to leave behind obstacles that prevented us from experiencing freedom from our mind and body.

We were into the third day when I started to experience something very unusual. Whenever I would go into a "Focus 10" state (as Bob called it), I would feel all this sexual energy running up and down my body, along with large phallic symbols that seemed to be coming at me from out of nowhere. Along with this, I would find myself caught in some dark black void I couldn't find a way out of. The energy was pretty strong, and there was a part of me that just wanted to say, "Relax, Kathy, and just go with it," but it just didn't feel like my stuff. I didn't know where it was coming from, especially since sex was the furthest thing from my mind during this workshop. It continued into the next sound training session as well, and it got even stronger. This really concerned me, and I went to discuss it privately with a trainer between sessions, hoping to better understand it. She seemed just as perplexed on how to advise me except to say: "Just push through it and see what happens." It was not the solution I sought.

After lunch, one of the male participants, a businessman in his early 40's named John, took me aside and asked if he could talk to me privately about something. I nodded, not at all prepared for what I was about to hear.

"A few of us overheard you talking to Melissa about what you were experiencing," he began. "I don't mean to upset you, but I think I know why this is happening to you."

He then proceeded to tell me that a few of the men attending the workshop had found themselves attracted to me and had found themselves fantasizing about me during their training sessions. Because of this distraction, they had decided to put me in their "energy conversion box" before embarking into other states of consciousness. I couldn't believe what I heard. Was he joking with me? I was no femme fatale. Granted, I was the youngest of the group's three women, but I hadn't even flirted with any guy there. I was married. Was my friendliness being misinterpreted?

"You're serious?" I asked, finding it really hard to believe that a few men's thought processes and fantasies could have such a powerful effect on my experience.

He nodded. "Yes. Sorry." He hesitated. "I can see I've upset you."

Damn right he had upset me. I was angry that their needs had put me into all these black voids where I experienced such utter confusion. Had I been wiser, I should have been wondering how and why I was so sensitive that I was picking up "their stuff" in the first place. I was more focused on feeling resentment that they were ruining my time because they couldn't control their thoughts.

My first instinct was to get even with them—teach them a lesson. But just as that thought took form, another one took its place. "Use it," I heard in my mind. "Learn something from it." The next thought I had was, "What do I want to learn?" and the answer came back quite clearly, "I want to experience unconditional love."

I went into the next training session with that goal in mind. I had never experienced that kind of love in any relationship up until that time. Back at home, my marriage was unraveling, and I sensed it was nearing its expiration date. Steve was a good man, but I had, in a sense, outgrown him as I sought answers beyond the physical realm. I felt incomplete as I craved deeper truth and knowledge.

Not long after crawling into my CHEC unit and hearing Bob's voice start to guide us through the focus states, I made my request known to the Universe. I wanted to feel what it felt like to be a part of universal love, to join with that part of me that existed in all things and everyone--to be spiritually and consciously connected. With those thoughts, I felt an implosion of energy build, and then I shot right out of my body through the top of my head. My intention, made pure and simple, served to open the doorway to the very realm I wanted to explore.

It was the fastest exit imaginable after two days of struggling for it to happen without any success. I felt myself floating outside my room and down the corridor of the ranch where participants' rooms were lined up on each end. I had no idea who was in what room, but I peeked into several, sending seeds of love and blessings to the males inside their CHEC units. I didn't know what I was supposed to do, nor should do, in this kind of experience, so I simply enjoyed feeling body-less on my quest to experience unconditional love. I figured whatever was meant to happen would happen.

Then it did. I found myself being pulled by a powerful force towards one particular room, then right into the CHEC unit of a young, rather good-looking, psychologist from Kansas. His eyes flew open in surprise, and it was if he could actually see me in my physical form above him. Of all the men at the workshop, this was one I had barely talked to. Whenever I tried, it was like there was a wall up. I figured he didn't like me for some reason, and so I left him alone. We seemed to be aware of each other, but for some unknown reason purposely avoided each other.

I had the sudden all-knowing that his vibrations were my vibrations. I floated over him and had an instantaneous flash of images of previous lifetimes we'd had together. From what I saw, I knew we had intimately known each other in the past in different forms: friend to friend, wife to husband, mother to child. I had an overwhelming desire to meld energies, to feel a part of him, to become one. And as I did, it was an experience that is beyond words, for love, total and absolute, surrounded us more strongly than one can ever experience and/or imagine. The more I gave, the greater I received. As the energy surged, it then rocked and exploded like some great astral orgasm. With it, came a feeling of completeness and connection, but an even greater experience of spiritual love. I remember thinking later how even the best orgasm paled in comparison. On some levels, it was also a meeting of minds and connection of souls.

My astral self could hear Bob, over the intercom, bringing us back from our exploratory session and back to full wakefulness. My physical body was still back in my own CHEC unit down the hall. With this realization, I was sucked right back to my body, and I didn't want to move. Or rather, I couldn't move. I was floating in bliss. At that moment, I felt complete.

Someone had to come and pull me out of my CHEC unit and bring me downstairs to the meeting room where, with the other workshop participants, we processed our experiences after each session. By the time I joined them, everyone seemed to be in a heightened energy state, talking excitedly. I glanced over at the young psychologist I had merged with and saw him talking with another man quite animatedly. He then stopped, looked directly at me, and silently mouthed ecstatically, "Thank you, thank you, thank you!"

There is always the skeptical part of you who wonders if you made the whole thing up. Was the experience just a figment of an over-active imagination? Was it a dream? It didn't feel like a dream. It was much too vivid. I had to find out. I walked up to him and asked him to tell me what he had experienced, because it was obvious whatever it was he was profoundly affected by it just as I was. I asked him if he wouldn't mind writing it down first, as would I. Our stories fit like puzzle pieces, just from different perspectives. I had no idea he also had full awareness of all his senses during the experience—the strongest being touch. He told me how shocked he was to suddenly see me appear in his CHEC unit. He, too, thought he might have imagined the whole experience.

So "Ask and you shall receive" has been a rather good truism for me. I wanted to experience spiritual love, and I got it. And in experiencing it, it opened yet another level for me of creative expression that would take me further along my destined path.

By the end of the week, I was experiencing a state of ego-less cosmic consciousness where I felt connected to everything. At first, this was not the most comforting experience, because with the loss of ego we lose what we feel is our identity. And without what we think is our identity, we feel lost and have to question who and what we are—and why we are here. A less strong mind might have slid right into psychosis. I took long walks, trying to make sense of who I thought I was. As I was walking down the road that led up to the ranch, a black cat jumped out of the brush and started to walk along beside me. I looked down at the cat, and he looked up at me. I started to jog along and so did the cat. I stopped jogging, and the cat stopped as well. We stared at each other again and then, as clear as could be, I heard the cat telepathically say: "You think too much. Don't worry. Bob will be along any minute and help you." And with that, the cat vanished back into the brush and was gone. I stopped and stared.

Oh. My. God. Now I was talking to animals! I had really lost it. Just as I wondered about my mental state, I heard a car coming around the bend in the road, and it was Bob Monroe just like the cat predicted. He stopped and asked if I wanted a ride back to the ranch. I thanked him and got in. I silently stared ahead, still thinking.

"You okay?" he asked.

"I'm not sure," I answered. "I just met a black cat who talked to me and told me you were coming."

Bob laughed and kept driving. "Oh, that was Blacky. He's quite a cat. He started showing up in my out-of-body travels one night and hasn't stopped. He's kind of an advanced animal soul."

I told Bob about my experiences thus far at the workshop, and later he would call and ask me if he could include the experience in a book he was writing called *Far Journeys*. I told him only if it could be published anonymously, which he assured me it would. So my experience is included there under 2312-CF, and this is the first time I am publically coming forward about it (although a few directors there know it was me). Twenty years later I returned to the Monroe Institute and found myself talking with a group sharing why they attended. One girl admitted, "I want to have an astral sex experience just like that girl did in *Far Journeys!*" A chorus of others agreed with her. I sat there silently, not admitting that was *my* experience, preferring to retain my anonymity. I couldn't help wondering how many people over the years had also signed up for the workshop based on wanting a similar experience. Bob Monroe is long gone, and his memory and work lives on, but I have to laugh at the thought that when I see him in the afterlife, I will remind him he probably owes me some sales commissions!

Kathy J. Forti, Ph.D.

Chapter 4
HIGHER EDUCATION

"Education is not preparation for life; education is life itself."
– JOHN DEWEY

Not long after returning from the Monroe Institute, I was filled with creative energy. I started writing, and the result was several mystical children's books dealing with issues such as death and dying, dreams, natural healing, and finding one's purpose in life. I had no idea if they had any merit or not. I had never written anything outside of a news story prior to that. So I sent them to my friend, Caroline Myss, and asked for her honest opinion. I knew she was an editor, but did not know she was an editor, at that time, for a new publisher in New Hampshire, called Stillpoint Publishing.

I don't think it was more than a week or two later she called me. "You're not going to believe this," she said. "But we just set up a children's division at Stillpoint, and we've been brainstorming about the type of story we'd like to publish. We thought it would be great if perhaps it was a story about a little boy or girl who met their spiritual guide, and they had adventures together. Then we received your book the next day, and the story was just as we had asked for."

I was shocked. Wow!

"And we want to publish it," she finished. Double wow!

Back in 1983 there were no other spiritual children's books outside of Leo Buscaglia's, *The Fall of Freddie the Leaf,* published a year earlier. I hadn't heard of his book at the time. His book dealt with dying in a more metaphorical sense, whereas mine dealt with real children's thoughts and ideas. It was published as three adventures under the title, *The Door to the Secret City,* but was thought to be progressively ahead of its time. Bookstores didn't have a category for spiritual children's books back in the 1980's. They didn't know whether to put such a selection in the adult section, where adults would be sure to buy it for their children, or on the children's shelves, where it was accurately categorized. Without a big mass marketing behind it, it got lost.

Stillpoint was a small publisher and the book didn't make it past a first initial printing. Later, I would buy back the rights, add three more metaphysical stories to it and e-book publish it under the title, *Freddie Brenner's Mystical Adventures* (available for FREE download at www.RinnovoPress.com*).* It was initially written for the children at the NYC Ronald McDonald House for their library, but I really wanted it to always be easily available to help inspire children everywhere at no cost.

Despite its modest showing in the publishing world, it managed to somehow get in the hands of therapists and hospice workers dealing with death and dying--which I came to realize was the true intent behind its creation. I soon found myself being asked to speak to groups of therapists and teachers on how to explain death and dying to children. I marvel at this now, because I was clearly no expert and didn't represent myself to be one, but they seemed to think I possessed such an expertise. It served to open doors for me, and before long, the people I lectured began asking, "Where's your practice?" or "What's your licensure?" They mistakenly thought I was already on their academic and professional level.

And that's how I got intimidated into going for my masters in counseling psychology at Old Dominion University in Virginia, before later moving on to get my doctorate. At first, I thought I needed the additional alphabet soup after my name to satisfy other people's need for academic credibility, but what I soon learned was that I was being led towards my true nature-- becoming a therapist and helping others. The little girl in me that had initially wanted to be a nurse found her calling.

Right out of graduate school, I got a job working at Norfolk Community Mental Health in Norfolk, Virginia, where I worked for several years before opening my own private practice. I became a Licensed Professional Counselor and Licensed Marriage & Family Therapist with an added specialty in neurofeedback and dissociative identity disorders. I attracted the unusual cases, and these patients would ultimately become my life teachers.

Working with dissociative identity disorders is where I truly learned to think outside the box with regard to the human psyche. Years ago, this disorder was called "Multiple Personality Disorder" (MPD) before it was then re-classified in the DSM-IV (*Diagnostic and Statistical Manual of Mental Disorders*) with the newer, less controversial title "Dissociative Identity Disorder" (DID). Like most therapists, I thought it was a rare condition I'd probably never see. How wrong I was. During my early days at Norfolk Community Mental Health, I was assigned a female patient who had a thick file with multiple diagnoses given to her by a string of social workers and therapists over the years in different cities and states. I had never seen so many diagnoses for one patient. No one seemed to agree on what was wrong with her, other than she was anxious and depressed. Valerie was a 40-year-old woman with seizure disorders, who had a long history of sexual, physical, and emotional abuse by multiple family members from infancy on. In order to receive medication and social services in Norfolk, she had to agree to counseling.

Valerie was one of my very first clients. From looking over her file, I knew this would not be a simple case. Quite frankly, I didn't know where to begin. Her history seemed so daunting, and I was still a novice therapist. I could tell she had been through a hundred first interviews before having been in the mental health system for years. She seemed so shy and reticent and resigned to her fate of having to be there in my office that I decided to just spend a little time talking about what brought her to Virginia and hopefully put her at ease. She had been sitting on the edge of her seat since she first sat down, like she was ready to spring towards the door at any moment, if warranted.

As I sat there talking with her, I noticed her glance over a few times at the toys and playthings I had on a shelf in the corner. At the time, I also ran a pre-school prevention program at the center for young mothers at risk for child physical abuse, so I had lots of interactive tools for younger children. Valerie seemed to be especially drawn to a jumbo container of pastel pencils and a drawing board easel.

Abruptly, she looked away and started to wring her hands in her lap. Had I not been making direct eye contact at the time, I almost certainly would have missed the quick but subtle rapid blinking of her eyes. When I asked her if she was okay, she got up and started pacing and that's when a red flag went off in my head. I couldn't explain it but I knew her energy had changed. She felt different. Her eyes surveyed the room as if trying to figure out where she was and how she got there. To most eyes, she would have appeared as just another anxious woman in a therapist's office. And indeed, her file had already listed her as having generalized anxiety disorder.

I don't know what made me say it, but the next words out of my mouth were, "Hello. What's *your* name?" Her eyes got wide as if she had been caught red-handed, and she began looking towards the door. She looked like she might bolt. I continued in a more soothing voice. "My name is Kathy." I smiled and nodded over at the colored pencils. "Would you like to draw?" She bit her lip and nodded back. That was my first introduction to 6-year-old Valerie Jean, who the 40-year-old adult Valerie didn't know existed. Valerie Jean emerged because she loved to draw, and my colored pencil collection fascinated her and drew her out.

We can't even begin to fathom the complexity of the human mind. Over the course of our therapy, and later when I took her with me to my private practice where I would see her pro bono for years, she and others like her became my teachers. Dissociative Identity Disorder, which used to be called Multiple Personality Disorder, usually occurs before the age of seven as a direct response to repeated sexual, physical, and/or emotional abuse over a period of time. The personality is still developing before age seven, and under traumatic situations, parts of the self can splinter off into full-blown alter personalities or fragments that can hold one or more memories, and sometimes only a part of a memory or event.

A child's way of coping with such abuse is to protect the ego self by believing that it happened to someone else, not them, so it splits off the personality to keep the whole self in feeling safe. To believe otherwise would be too risk ego annihilation. When these individuals bring such a coping mechanism with them into adulthood, it becomes dysfunctional and usually leads to severe depression and anxiety—thereby landing them in the mental health system, or worse yet the prison system, if they outwardly express their depression as violence.

The key goal for the therapist is to gain the patient's trust and help them integrate all those lost parts of their self into a functional whole. My client, Valerie, had well over 100 personalities and alter parts, which I would discover over the years I treated her. Not a hint of her true diagnosis was ever found in her original case file, even though there had been some obvious clues all along. All of them went unnoticed, since most therapists may still be under the impression that such a diagnosis is very rare. Believe me, it isn't. There are a lot of very high functioning "multiples" out there, as they like to be called. Some of Valerie's alter parts were males, some were females of all ages. Some were pre-verbal (wild child) feral parts that had memories from infancy and could only do crude stick drawings of what happened, while other older alters had some amazing drawing skills. One or two alters even spoke a second language that others in their personality system didn't understand. Some were left-handed, while others were right-handed. Some alters needed glasses to read, others had perfect eyesight. Some had allergies, while others did not.

The numerous differences would comprise a long and very astounding list.

Not to get into a long discourse about this particular client, I mention her because she helped me to learn a lot about the power of the mind when it comes to healing. She always made me think about how little we know and understand. Whenever she was required to visit her OB-GYN for pap smears and routine gynecological tests, her doctor would always insist that I be there in the examination room. This is a very odd request for any therapist, and not something I would normally do. However, the first time she had gotten a routine gynecological exam by that doctor, a child alter had come out and thought she was being sexually abused. It triggered a full-scale abreaction (re-living of a past abuse), and my client started crying and screaming. She curled up in a corner to hide. It totally freaked out the doctor and his staff--and most assuredly his waiting room full of patients, who could hear her distress. This doctor did not want to risk such a thing ever happening again. So I was there to ground my client and make sure all the child alters were in a safe place inside the system, and only an older adult alter or the host personality was out for the duration of the exam. Usually, when I did this there were no incidents. My goal was to get her to eventually do this for herself, but in the beginning I helped her.

After one of these gynecological exams, the tests came back that Valerie had cervical cancer. An adult alter named Jeanie had been out and present that day during the exam. When my client went back for a follow-up exam and a different adult alter named B.B. was present, the test results showed no trace of cervical cancer at all. The doctor repeated the test several times, thinking perhaps the lab had somehow made an error. Yet in the end, when Jeanie was out, cancer was present. When B.B. was out, it wasn't there. At that point, the doctor scratched his head and went into his own state of denial. He couldn't explain it, and quite frankly, neither could I. It certainly gives one something to think about. Most people have a hard time wrapping their brain around such an anomaly. For me, it served as one of the catalysts to opening my mind to the possibility that health and disease are not set in concrete but fluctuate according to the thought and emotional patterns that make up the personality. Bruce Lipton, in his book *The Biology of Belief*, found from his own research studies that "beliefs control biology." In the words of Mahatma Gandhi: "Your beliefs become your thoughts; Your thoughts become your words; Your words become your actions; Your actions become your habits; Your habits become your values; Your values become your destiny."

In school, I was taught that the mind is the product of the brain. After my near-death experience, I knew that wasn't true. The brain is just a physical organism, a high-tech relay system much like a computer. On the other hand, the mind is the powerhouse behind thought, personality, and soul-driven purpose. It's the brain's master programmer and cannot be measured or found on CT-Scans or in anatomy books. This is because mind is the inherent link to our divineness. The MIND IS THE BUILDER.

I spent a lot of time studying the mind, and my patients became my teachers. I would see how, in the end, everything comes down to a matter of choice. You might be born into a seriously flawed body or brain organism, but it doesn't mean you have absolutely no control over what you say and do. I know some people will disagree with me on this. I saw patients that were severely depressed, almost suicidal, rein in these tendencies and act competently and responsibly when it was absolutely crucial—like seeing to a child's needs or safety. So I came to see that there is a split second when we are allowed to choose whether to give in and slide into psychosis or depression, or pull ourselves out of the darkness into the light. Again, the MIND IS THE BUILDER.

They say you practice what you most need to learn. I was practicing therapy to understand both myself and others. The foundation had been laid. I also believe when you have learned what you need to learn, a doorway is opened and you move on to the next learning phase.

Kathy J. Forti, Ph.D.

Chapter 5
RE-ENTRY

"What lies behind us and what lies before us are tiny matters compared to what lies within us." – RALPH WALDO EMERSON

My near-death experience in 2003 was the beginning of a new journey and learning phase for me. I tried to pick up the strands of a normal life after it happened, but it was clearly evident that door had already closed, and there was no turning back. A new life for me had begun, which would be filled with obstacles and tests like nothing I could have imagined. I had entered the research, and hopefully the promise of an enlightenment stage in my life.

I somehow knew my days doing therapy were numbered. Because of this, I was filled with anxiety, not knowing what I could possibly do instead to make a living. So not knowing what to do, I just stuck it out. At first, I didn't tell my family what had happened to me. I knew my mother and sister would worry about my health and pressure me to get all kind of tests, thinking I was headed for a fatal heart attack. I didn't want to deal with their anxiety as well.

My father, on the other hand, had always been like a rock for me. One summer, when I was about seven years old, I used to get inexplicable daily nose bleeds. My father was the one to reassure me he had gone through the same thing when he was a boy, and maybe it was just hereditary. They were "gushers," as my sister called them. I could go through a whole box of tissue or a toilet paper roll whenever it occurred. My mother would panic at the sight of blood, subconsciously fearing I was bleeding to death. My father, though, was calm and collected and weathered me through the ordeal, joking and telling me stories. I definitely preferred him in attendance during nose bleed times, and my mother was more than happy to hand this duty over to him. So it was only natural that my father was the first family member I would share my near-death experience with, a month later, in June 2003.

I remember him quietly listening to me re-tell what had occurred. He smiled and said, "That's very interesting," before finally adding, "but I'm glad you're still here." He made no further comments or judgments about anything I said, and I figured that was that. At heart, my father was always a pretty supportive guy.

On July 1, 2003, less than a month later, he died. No one saw it coming. My parents had built a lakefront vacation home in Elkhorn, Wisconsin, on Lauderdale Lakes. My father designed and built their house, which was a multi-tiered circular construction. It was such an unusual design, that locals referred to it as the "Round House" on the lake. A constant parade of pontoon boats passed by it during summertime, as lake residents slowed their motors to show their friends the unusual house that Roy Forti built. At night the house looked like a well-lit, rather large, flying saucer. My father was proud of his 12-year home-building project—especially having had no formal design and construction training. He loved puttering around on his land, so it was only fitting that it should also be the setting for his end-of-life departure.

Always steady on his feet and sure-footed, he suffered a head fall climbing the stairs alongside his beloved boathouse. Despite having also broken his hip in the fall, he seemed relatively fine and was even talking. But local medical staff decided to airlift him to a head trauma unit at a Milwaukee hospital, just to play it safe. That night, he died of a brain aneurysm in his sleep. I remember being awakened in the middle of the night to receive the news from my sister in New York City. I was devastated. Up until that point in my life, I had had no one of real significance die. I couldn't help but wonder at the timing of what I had revealed to my father about my own near-death experience only a month earlier. Had I known he would soon be departing this world so soon after our talk, would I have said or done anything differently? You can second-guess yourself to death, but I had no idea if anything I said had made a difference during his own transition.

I wasn't given the luxury of pondering what I had or had not done. Death means taking care of an endless stream of details, and my mother left it to me and my siblings to make the appropriate arrangements. You learn fast what needs to be done whether you want to or not.

Much later, I would come to fully understand why I had told only my father about my near-death experience. On a conscious level, I didn't know he was preparing to die, but on a soul level I did, and he needed to hear what happened to me. This became evident about a month after his death.

I happened to be talking to my friend, E.M. "Gene" Nicolay, once again on the phone. It was a casual, friendly call to connect and catch up when suddenly he interrupted me. "Kathy, your father is here." I thought he was joking and laughed, "Oh, I didn't know you also channeled dead people." But he was serious.

"He's really here and he says he has something he needs to tell you."

A part of me needed to make sure it was my father. "What's he look like?" Gene had never met or seen a photo of my father, so I figured it was a fair question. I was stunned when he accurately described him.

"He says to tell you that you were right."

"About what?" I had no idea what that meant. One doesn't usually hear one's deceased parent come back to tell them they were right. That's when I learned that my father had supportively listened to me telling him about my near-death experience, but all along, he thought I must have dreamed it up. Instead of ridiculing or challenging me on the experience, he had merely nodded, smiled, and paid me lip service that what I described was indeed "interesting." I was shocked that, all along, he thought what I was saying was crazy, and he hadn't believed it. But when he passed over in death, he remembered my words and wanted me to know he knew what to do and what it was all about. So, indeed, it was important for him to tell me "thank you" and that I was right. This was followed by messages for other family members that would help them through this difficult time, which Gene hadn't previously known.

My near-death experience served to be a preparation for not only me, but my father as well. Once again, I was someone else's messenger. Yet, oddly enough he turned out to also be my messenger. After he died, he would make the carved wooden clock chime in my parents' living room whenever he was around. This regulator clock was shaped like a violin and sat atop a grand piano. No one ever wound this particular clock (it was quite noisy), and it sat there like a forgotten decorative piece. He managed to manipulate it when family members were around. Later, when my mother died, not to be outdone by my father, she chose a different clock in the house, one with a glass-globed mechanism, which was her favorite, and she would make it spin and spin. I come from a very competitive family. It was their way of saying, "We're still with you."

Years later, when I was visiting my Aunt Jo in Chicago for the Thanksgiving holiday, my mother managed to make a never-wound music box play in the hallway by the living room. My aunt, my cousin, and I all heard the music and said in unison, "What's that?" Immediately it stopped playing. There were a few music boxes on the shelf, and I asked my aunt which one my mother had given her. The second she pointed to the Christmas scene from my mother, it started playing again. "It's Mom," I said, with a delighted smile. We sat back down and, as soon as we did, the music box started playing again. Not once, but three times is certainly validation to me. For some reason, spirits seem to be quite adept at manipulating small wind-up objects. They are giving us signs all the time; we just have to be open and accepting.

Kathy J. Forti, Ph.D.

Chapter 6
RESEARCH & ENLIGHTENMENT

"The only source of knowledge is experience." – *ARISTOTLE*

I felt lost after my father died. It took about a month for it to set in that my Rock of Gibraltar was gone and was not coming back. My father was the life of the party, always smiling, joking, and everyone sought him out to "fix" things. Despite living through the Great Depression and experiencing an impoverished childhood after his father died when he was two years old, he still managed to overcome obstacles and rise above others who had more than his limited high school education. I remember once asking him if he had ever been so down or depressed that he had contemplated ending his life. It was a risky question to ask a parent, but he always seemed so positive I had to know if he had ever gone through a dark night of his soul.

He didn't scoff or dismiss such a question. He simply thought about it for a moment and said, "No, because I know there is always more than one solution to every problem. You just have to be open to seeing it." Those words stuck with me, especially during the years ahead that would test me in every conceivable way. I guess life is all about how you handle "Plan B."

Not long after my father's passing, my mother's breast cancer returned after almost 10 years in remission. She tried to hide the extent of it so as not to put even more pressure on her kids, thereby weathering a lot of it alone. As a therapist, I had long ago discovered that my breast cancer patients had similar tendencies. They tended to nurture everyone but themselves and, energetically, disease manifested in the part of the body most associated with nurturing—the breasts. My mother was no different. She loved her children fiercely, but she held in old anger and resentments from years past and had difficulty letting go. But one can never be a therapist to another family member. If I pushed my mother too hard hoping to help her, she would simply say, "Stop with all that psycho-babble shit." For her to say "shit" meant she was really mad. My mother rarely swore, and I never ever heard her say the f*** word in her entire life. I learned to back off and accept that this was her life's journey and her decisions, and I needed to honor her choices, whatever they were.

It was her reoccurrence of breast cancer that directed my thoughts back to a wider view of healing. I found myself drawn to all kinds of books on energy psychology and alternative medicine. My book pile grew as I tried to absorb what others had learned. During this process, I was aware of being guided about which books to read and which ones to ignore. If it was something I didn't need to read, I would immediately fall asleep during the first few pages. On the other hand, if it was on track for me, I couldn't sleep until I devoured the book. This meant I was up all night reading. I felt like I was on a truth-seeking mission with manic reading tendencies. I had replaced my post-near-death experience early physics fascination on the Internet with the world of energy healing literature instead.

That's where I first learned about Rife technology. Royal Raymond Rife had a very fascinating story, and it was hard to believe no one has ever made a movie about his life--probably because most people have never heard of him, and I'm sure the American Medical Association and Big Pharma would prefer to keep it that way.

In the 1920's, Dr. Royal Raymond Rife, a John Hopkins University trained microbiologist, invented the first Universal Microscope which, for the first time, allowed researchers to observe living organisms without killing them--unlike electron microscopes. Electron microscopes allowed scientists to see mold, parasites, and bacteria, but not observe live viruses, which was crucial to understanding their ever-changing, morphing behavior.

While building his high-powered microscope, Rife, through pain-staking hours of observation, observed that each organism had their own unique signature frequency at which they vibrated and thrived. With further experimentation, he was also able to discover what frequency they couldn't thrive at and would ultimately eradicate them. This led to his development of a frequency device to kill harmful organisms that contributed to disease.

Rife was the first who succeeded in isolating the virus specific to cancer and conducted over 400 experiments with cancerous tumors in mice before experimenting on human cancers. He made up charts showing which frequency settings would destroy which microbe or virus, and these are still used today. The news of his work quickly spread, and many articles and news stories appeared documenting his accomplishments. Physicians in

Southern California began hearing of Rife's work and came to observe and verify his results. Forty-four Los Angeles area physicians came to honor him at a banquet reception in November 1931 and heralded him as the man who discovered the way to "end all disease."

In 1934, the University of Southern California appointed a Special Medical Research Committee to bring 16 terminally ill patients from the Pasadena County Hospital to Rife's lab in San Diego for a 90-day treatment program using Rife's recommended frequencies. The team included doctors and pathologists assigned to examine the patients upon completion of treatment. Fourteen of the patients were declared free of cancer after 90 days, and the two remaining patients required an additional 30 days of treatment to be completely cured.

In 1939, Rife was formally invited to address the Royal Society of Medicine in London, England, which had verified his findings. He was even praised by the Smithsonian Institute in a 1944 article they published.

Due to all the publicity and accolades Rife received, the head of the American Medical Association (AMA), a man named Morris Fishbein, tried to purchase the exclusive rights to Rife's invention. When Rife turned him down, physicians using his treatment program were threatened by the AMA and the State of California with the loss of their medical licenses. By 1939, most of the doctors and scientists working with Rife denied they had ever met him. Arthur Kendall, the Director of the Northwestern School of Medicine who worked with Rife on the cancer virus, accepted almost a quarter a million dollars to suddenly retire to Mexico. Dr. George Dock was silenced with an enormous grant along with AMA honors. Others went back to prescribing drugs. As for Rife, Fishbein made sure he was embroiled in lawsuits that would financially bankrupt him and bury his technology forever. The AMA made sure its use would forever be banned in the United States and no longer be able to threaten the international pharmaceutical industry. Rife died in 1971 at the age of 83, a penniless man.

I found out I could easily obtain the Rife technology in Canada, and being very curious, I bought a device to see what it could do. It looked very similar to a CB radio where you could dial certain frequencies. An argon gas tube attached to the device and pulsated a pinkish light when the frequencies were transmitted.

My mother was the first to try it. I couldn't gauge how effective it might be unless I saw the cancerous area before we started. It was the first time she allowed me to see what her breast area looked like. Her left breast had been removed years ago (something she also failed to tell us). She had informed us that she had a partial lumpectomy, not a radical removal of her entire breast. The truth was now unavoidable, and I tried not to look completely shocked by the blackish tissue now visible where her breast used to be. She would put pads on it to dress the surrounding tissue that periodically seeped a clear fluid. It looked nasty. She was seeing a physician, but refused to go the chemotherapy and radiation route. She believed if she had beaten it once years ago through only macrobiotics and a strict change in diet, she could do it again. She was now in her 80's and I was not so sure.

After a few weeks of Rife treatments where she would sit in front of the frequency machine for one to two hours a day, the black tissue around her breast area slowly turned to a reddish pink, then fleshy pink. Her nails started becoming healthy looking, where before they were brittle and ridged. She had renewed energy and stamina. Even the color in her cheeks improved. Something was happening. Even her physician noticed, but she failed to tell him what she was doing differently, for fear of being ridiculed. I left the device with her in Chicago and encouraged her to keep using it.

In the meantime, I decided to get another Rife device to experiment with in California. I wasn't even sure how I was going to use it, since it was against the law in California and other states to use it on patients. But I was curious and wanted to know more. That's when I came across a handbook on Rife frequencies, which listed the frequencies that were adverse to different diseases and helped eradicate them. Interestingly enough, there was a section in the book on frequencies for emotional conditions. That got my attention. I had assumed that Rife addressed strictly physical conditions. But there it was—the frequencies for depression and anxiety. Would they work?

That's when I was divinely inspired. I wondered what would happen if one put names in front of the Rife device while it was running. Would it do anything? I immediately thought of two new male clients I had begun seeing that week, both clearly depressed and anxious. I wrote their names on a piece of paper. Then, I wondered what it would feel like if I also received the treatment, feeling a little moody that day myself. I was not depressed or anxious, but my curiosity was always up for an experiment.

I sat down in front of the Rife device, dialed up the frequencies to reduce depression and anxiety, but before I hit the Run switch, I picked up the piece of paper with the two male clients' names. I figured we'd all get the treatment together, so I taped their names to my chest and sat back in the chair. I heard my own inner Guides say loud and clear "Are you sure you really want to do that?" I foolishly ignored the subtle warning. I didn't think anything untoward could possibly happen. After all, I was just having fun experimenting.

It was a 30-minute session. I quietly read a book throughout it, while the pulsing frequencies did their thing. I felt nothing throughout the session. About 15-20 minutes afterward, it hit me like nothing I could have expected. I suddenly felt like someone had given me an extreme dose of testosterone and with it came the most bizarre sexual addiction I could have imagined. I was obsessed with insatiable thoughts of sex. Visions and overwhelming desires of cruising Internet porn sites, looking for specific images, seized me.

However embarrassing this is to tell about, the fact was that all I could think about was sex, and more sex. A part of me was observing this whole process and wondering what the hell had happened to me. Could it have had something to do with those names on the paper I had taped to my chest during the session? I had no way of knowing. I decided to re-run the same session on myself, but this time without the names. Miraculously, within a short time after the session, the sexual addiction abated, then totally disappeared. I still was clueless why I had manifested such symptoms in the first place.

This experimentation happened over the weekend. On Monday, I returned to my therapy practice and had a session with one of the males whose name I had written on the piece of paper attached to my chest. I asked him how he had been fairing since our first session.

He looked at me quite enthusiastically and said, "This is the first weekend I felt free of my sexual addiction." Whoa, I thought. He hadn't told me anything about a sexual addiction in our first meeting. He also hadn't told me he was gay, and that he had a porn addiction where he cruised adult sites every night.

I wasn't about to tell him, "Yes, I know exactly how you feel." I wasn't sure how I had taken on his addiction, nor could I explain it scientifically, but the fact remained, I had. It got me to wondering if we are all just human energetic transmitting and receiving stations. Sometimes what we pick up is obvious, and sometimes it's not.

Because of this experience, I have great empathy for males and the male libido. If I had to deal with testosterone-induced sex thoughts all day long, I don't know how I would get any work done. My hat goes off to all you males reading this. Females could never understand this without experiencing it firsthand.

The point of this rather personal and revealing story is that energy can be transmitted, and information can be easily received from one source to another or, in this case, person-to-person. Since my near-death experience, I felt my clients' emotions more strongly than ever. Now, it seemed I was even picking up desires and compulsions from clients, which I hadn't had any prior knowledge of. When this occurs, it certainly gives you something to think about. I knew it was very significant. It was clear to me that strong sexual experiences are key factors in bringing about psi experiences. There seems to be little difference in whether psychic openings stem from a traumatic or non-traumatic event, if the emotional impact is significant enough. This certainly was true for me and would continue to repeat itself, which I'll explain more in depth later (Chapter 17, Psychic-Sexual Triggers).

After this experience, I was intrigued with how an energy device could somehow facilitate my becoming a brief surrogate for my client's unknown addiction, thereby helping him to find relief. I recalled seeing the 1980 movie *Resurrection*, where after a near-death experience the character, played by Ellen Burstyn, discovers she has the ability to heal people's physical infirmities by taking on their illnesses. Perhaps there were many ways to affect this same phenomenon.

I wondered if anyone else had used the Rife machine like I had, using names as proxy for the real person, so I tracked down the author of the Rife frequency handbook and asked her myself. She was intrigued with my story and results, but said she had never heard anyone using it in such a manner. We talked for a while, and she mentioned other energetic devices I might want to check out. She gave me the name of a friend in Los Angeles to contact, named Nadia (not her real name), who had a device she was using from an inventor in Europe. The device was very expensive, complicated to use, and was also based on frequencies like the Rife machine. I felt compelled to check it out, much as I had felt compelled to learn about other energy devices out there. It didn't do much for me personally, but I was told the inventor was brilliant. I felt that if I was indeed intended to help develop a health-related technology, then I should be looking for the right people with expertise to help me.

I told Nadia about my near-death experience, and the information I had been receiving, and she wanted to be a part of it. I suggested we go see the inventor in Hungary and see if he would be interested in working with us on this new device. He was an eccentric-type person who seemed to like our concept for an energetic anti-aging type technology, but told us he wouldn't work with us unless we put down an $85,000 deposit. Nadia didn't have any money, so foolishly I paid it all myself to get the project started. He proposed it would be based on his existing technology, the information on which he wouldn't share with anyone.

As soon as the relationship with this inventor began, my Guides became very quiet. I assumed their silence meant I was finally doing what they wanted me to do and was on the right track, helping bring this new device forward into the world. But from the moment I agreed to work with this inventor, disruptive obstacles occurred on every front. Nadia wanted half ownership in the device without putting up any money or doing the creative work, and the inventor stalled for six months before showing us what he called a prototype. When he finally sent us his prototype software, I was shocked that it looked exactly like his existing device with a change in color only. He hadn't even looked at any of my designs or layout. After another six months of stalling and constant overseas phone calls to his office trying to see where he was and never being able to locate him, I knew I had been had. I demanded my money back, having received nothing after a year. I never got back all my monies, and my relationship with Nadia soured after being stuck with corporate legal bills we were supposed to share equally. It was a very expensive lesson, but one I hadn't completely learned yet. (Later I would learn that he had waited me out until I had enough of his stalling in order to co-produce the concept with a Canadian company at a bigger profit for himself. He had clearly violated our legal contracts, but I decided that a legal action would only tie me to that negative energy even longer. Instead, I opted to cut my losses and move on. A few years later, the Canadian company was facing bankruptcy due to corporate misuse of funds and illegal activities. So karma often does take care of these things in the end.)

Six months into the debacle with the inventor in Hungary, I started winding down my therapy practice, thinking I would focus on preparing myself to give my energies totally to the new device I thought I was developing. After calling it quits with him, I was very short on finances and didn't know if I should go back to re-building my therapy practice or building this dream with someone else. Then my mother died. She decided she had had enough of treatment and therapies, and we had to honor her decision. She was 81 when she died on December 12, 2004, a year and a half after my father's passing. She was on a respirator and was intubated her last two days in the hospital. She kept lapsing in and out of consciousness and couldn't speak, but she managed to scrawl a few words on a paper that said, "It hurts too much. I quit." I was shocked to see these words. By nature she was a fighter and had always boasted that she was determined to live to 126. I knew she had had enough and was giving us permission to take her off life support. As we sat by her hospital bedside, I heard my Guides tell me very clearly that it was time to stop touching her. Doing so was holding her to the earth plane. It was difficult not holding her hand or smoothing her forehead, but we did. Hours later, she passed. After both of your parents have died, you feel like an orphan. You are no one's baby any more. You are an adult on your own, and your parental fan club is permanently gone.

For the last year of her life, my siblings and I had taken turns going home to Chicago so someone would be there with her every weekend to give her home health care worker a break. It took its toll on everyone, but we wanted to be there for her like she had always been there for each of us. In 2003, I lost my father; in 2004, I lost my mother, most of my savings, and most of my therapy practice. I didn't know what to do or where I was going.

I tried again, thinking I had just found the wrong inventor to work with and perhaps needed to keep looking. Someone introduced me to another inventor here in the United States, who also seemed quite brilliant. He only asked for $15,000 up front, which seemed like a bargain after the last inventor. He also worked with frequencies and had built software programs. None of his programs were well known, but he was willing to give my ideas a shot, and he seemed more accessible. But just like the first inventor, as soon as I made the commitment to start working together, the obstacles began all over again. He did the exact same thing as the first inventor. He stalled for quite a while, then showed me a prototype that was nothing like I had asked for. I couldn't even figure out how to navigate it. The nightmare was happening all over again. I refused to give him more money to go any further, and I was back to square one again. My Guides, like before, were strangely quiet throughout this second learning lesson.

I was so frustrated and confused at these repeated failures I just wanted to curl up in a ball and die. Was I delusional, I wondered? I doubted myself and everything that had happened to me. I was angry with myself and fearful of the situation I found myself in. I raged at my silent Guides, "I give up! I don't know what you want from me."

Pema Chodron, a Buddhist Monk, who wrote *When Things Fall Apart: Heart Advice for Difficult Times,* said: "Fear is a natural reaction to moving closer to the truth." That's when I heard, quite clearly, with a level of infinite patience, my Guides deliver my words of truth, "We don't want *them* to do this. We want *you* to do it."

I thought I *was* doing "it." I sat down on the floor and quietly listened and waited. "You are unlimited," they began. "You already have all the knowledge within you to create what you desire." The problem was they might have thought so, but I didn't. I had sought out other scientists thinking they were certainly more capable and smarter than I was, and I wasn't totally convinced I had the ability to carry out the depth of this task. They seemed to be telling me I needed to trust in the process. I had gotten burned twice already, and trust was not something I had a lot of at that time. But this was a part of my journey—to learn to trust myself and to trust my own inner guidance.

I was left alone to contemplate this mission I had agreed to. I struggled with it. I feared further failure and disappointment. Losing hard-earned money certainly helped to put things into a more narrow perspective. You learn to be more cautious and discerning. They waited me out—never forcing the issue. I had the freedom of choice, yet I still felt something driving me forward. I felt like there was a time factor at stake, and I had already used a good portion of it trying to get others to do the work. I knew what I would and would not do, but I also knew that my decision could not be put off indefinitely. I slept on it and the next morning felt I had finally reached a juncture. I knew I had to make my choice, and that choice would mean a commitment and an even bigger learning curve.

There was no turning back. I'd do my best, even though I didn't know what that might entail. Had I known at the time all that I would struggle with later, I might have run in the opposite direction. Nevertheless, I made my decision and, with it, I suddenly felt like a great weight had been lifted from my heart— quite possibly shifting to my shoulders instead.

"I need help," I thought. Within hours after I accepted taking on this mission, it was like a door opened in my mind and new concepts came flooding in fast and furious. They came in all forms. Some were visual pictures, some auditory instructions, and some concepts came down in whole chunks like downloads of information to my brain. Most of it I had no prior conscious knowledge of, despite the fact that my Guides assured me I had known this information for centuries and was just re-learning what was necessary for this project. When I realized what they were opening up to me, I knew immediately why they had not shared this knowledge while I was trying to work with the other inventors. They wanted to usher in a whole new and different technology that would indeed change people's concept about healing. I would soon understand exactly what that meant.

Kathy J. Forti, Ph.D.

Chapter 7
MAKING A DIFFERENCE

"The purpose of life is a life of purpose." – ROBERT BYRNE

Every human being and creature on earth is consciously connected. Everything is made up of energy, and we all come from
the same energy source that created the planets and the universe.
Whether you call it God, Buddha, Allah, Christ, or the Source--
we are still all part of the One or Whole. Change by one person
in the Whole can have a trickle-down effect, whether intended or
not. I witnessed this with my therapy patients. If one cog in the
family system does a self-correction, then eventually the rest of
the system adjusts to it and creates a state of balance or homeo-
stasis. They may fight the change at first, trying to return to what
feels comfortable and familiar; but if the person making the
change is consistent in behavior and belief, the change can
ultimately affect not just one person, but also an entire family.
Taking it to a higher level, it can change an entire species, or a
nation, even a planet.

Back in 1988, I had already learned that one person *can* make
a change heard round the world--especially if they are trying to
correct a wrong, whether it be to another person, or society as a
whole. I didn't consciously intend to make the change that
occurred at that time, but nevertheless it happened (which I will
explain shortly). When I started working on developing this new
technology, my Guides reminded me again and again of the

influence one voice or action could have in affecting fellow human beings and quite possibly expand a universal belief system. It was an important theme.

They showed me snippets of my own history, to support where I'd been, in connection to where I was now headed. In May of 1988, I spent three days at a therapeutic breath workshop in Key Largo, Florida. The facilitators were instructing participants in using breathing to tap into creative intuitive states. Quite frankly, I wasn't much interested in learning how to breathe, since I already seemed to be doing okay on my own in that department. The real reason I signed up for the workshop was because part of it entailed swimming with the dolphins in a Key Largo facility. I lived in Virginia Beach, Virginia, at the time, and each summer I had watched schools of bottle-nosed dolphins frolic in the waters off the Atlantic Coast. Like many of my generation, I grew up watching the TV series *Flipper*. So, of course, I envisioned an idyllic human and mammal experience like Luke and his family did. I longed to join these creatures, understand their world, and communicate man's desire to be friends. I was terribly naive. What I encountered instead was something that would re-construct my beliefs about man and his imposition on nature.

The dolphin-swim facility I visited was a series of fenced-in pens built off a natural canal leading to the ocean. Each pen held three dolphins, and four humans were allowed into a pen during each swim session. The dolphins circled close to the dive platform, eyeing each of us curiously as we donned our snorkeling gear.

I was a certified diver at the time and felt quite comfortable in the water. I dove in without prompting. Visibility was poor. My heart skipped a beat as something brushed up against my leg. A larger-than-life, 500-pound mammal brushed up against me. I paid close attention to the sonar sounds they emit to get a bearing on what direction they were coming from. Another one swam right under me. I dove down to swim with it, but it was gone with a powerful thrust of its tail.

Prior to getting in the water, the facility owners had given us a brief orientation telling us how "amorous and playful" the dolphins were and to just "go with it." They never explained what this really meant. Seconds later, I heard a dolphin come up behind me, then without warning I felt my leg being grabbed and forcefully shaken. It increased in intensity, and I found myself pulled down further under the surface without air support. I thought I was under some kind of attack. I saw, to my astonishment, that it was a male dolphin and he was trying to mate. His penis had dropped down from inside his body and wrapped itself around my kneecap. The more I tried to get away, the more he latched on. This did not feel "amorous and playful" to me. I had to kick the hell away from him. The dolphin's aggressiveness confused me. In my mind, I screamed, "Now, Stop it!" and he eased off enough for me to start heading back to the dive platform.

I was not the only woman this dolphin acted out on. One woman was so upset she tried to get out of the water, only to have the dolphin grab her scuba fin and attempt to pull her back in. I knew instinctively that this was the behavior of a frustrated animal in captivity. The dolphin's name was "Fonzie" and this was certainly no *Happy Days* experience. I learned after the fact that this same adolescent dolphin had a long history of such aggressive behavior, which strangely didn't seem to concern staff personnel or the owners.

The facility was sanctioned as a research center where even handicapped and autistic children could come to interact and have a "healing experience" with the dolphins. I wondered what kind of experience a child would take away from such an encounter. It raised a lot of troubling questions for me. I recognized that the dolphins were being subjected to at least four 30-minute human swim programs a day. The program had a steady stream of paying customers, and the facility was bringing in a sizable income from these programs. As a self-proclaimed research center, I also wondered at the validity of any research data that is obtained from animals penned up and subjected to a steady stream of human invaders. It would be the equivalent of some alien intelligence trying to accurately document the human race by studying prison inmates.

I quit the breath workshop and dolphin swim program that very day and did not go back to finish it. I knew instinctively that what I participated in was wrong, and the dolphins were trying to tell me this. *I want to be free!* Perhaps they picked the loudest mouth in the water pen that day, knowing on some level I would do something if they shook me up enough, and they were right.

Upon returning home, I wrote a three-page letter to the National Oceanic & Atmospheric Administration (NOAA) in Washington, D.C., urging them to stop granting permits to human-dolphin swim facilities, because it was morally and ethically wrong. A Hyatt Hotel in Hawaii had recently applied for such a permit, and NOAA was getting ready to render a decision whether to grant one or not. I sent a copy of the letter to Greenpeace, having heard they were also trying to actively shut down such facilities--a fact I had not known prior to my human-dolphin encounter. Had I known, I probably would have just seen them as "spoil sports." As I already admitted, I was very naive and misinformed. Yet, by writing the letter, I felt it was my responsibility to try and make my experience count and my voice heard.

What I didn't anticipate was my letter going viral. It was a well-written, three-page letter. I had no idea many mainstream newspapers, rag magazines, and TV news shows would eventually track me down wanting the story from "the girl who got raped by a dolphin." The first responders didn't even bother to contact me and went immediately for the sensational. I didn't catch wind that my story had hit the newsstands until a friend in New York, whom I hadn't heard from in a long time, called to ask if I was all right. When I questioned why she would ask, she told me she had been standing in a long supermarket line reading the Globe newspaper when she was horrified to come across my name in a story about dolphins. "It said Kathy Forti of Virginia Beach, Virginia, was raped by a dolphin!" This news equally horrified me. For several years afterward, I seemed to be the "go to contact" on every news Rolodex for dolphins-in-captivity stories. I refused all sensationalist offers and went only with those whose story might make a difference in making a change for these animals. I became friendly with former Navy dolphin trainers and learned that when in captivity, a dolphin's lifespan is short-ened by 50%. Due to the constant interactive stress with humans, most dolphins have ulcers and are given Tagamet to medicate them. And the little-known secret is they often exhibit aggressive behavior in the wild even to their own species, as was documented by researchers in the National Geographic film, *The Dark Side of Dolphins*.

To this day, I will not attend a dolphin or whale entertainment show. To swim with dolphins in the wild is one thing. There, they have a choice whether to interact or not with humans. In a pen, they usually don't get fish if they don't interact or perform. It's my opinion that swimming with dolphins in captivity is anything but spiritual; it's a paid-for water pony ride at the animal's expense. I know people will deny this and will rationalize doing so—maybe even dislike me for saying it, but it's still not right. No wild animal should ever be held captive.

As a result of the media attention and awareness my letter generated, human-dolphin swim permits for new facilities were stopped. There are countries in the world that ban cetacean entertainment altogether—India, Hungary, Costa Rica, and Chile. The United States should also be on that list, but as of this writing, it's not. The documentary movie *Blackfish* exposed the history of accidents and aggressive behavior by killer orca whales toward trainers at SeaWorld. One very experienced trainer was actually eaten, and her death led to other trainers deeply questioning if what they were doing with these large intelligent creatures was wrong.

So even though I digress here with my *Save-the-Dolphins-from-Captivity* story, it served to introduce me to the reality that one voice coupled with others could make a difference in changing the world. I had witnessed it firsthand without even consciously trying. I wondered if I could help make a greater difference, but this time by conscious intent.

When I was a child, my all-time favorite movie every Christmas season was Frank Capra's, *It's a Wonderful Life*. I waited and watched religiously for it to come on television every year even before it became a cult movie classic. It made quite an impact on me from the first time I saw Clarence the Angel show poor George Bailey how one person's life could have such a domino effect on so many other lives around him. I wanted to be like Jimmy Stewart's character, George Bailey, and know that I could also make a difference. Some of us just want to make it through life, while others of us hope that in the process we can make the world a better place. We hope to do something meaningful, even if we never learn who or how another person or persons will be impacted by our good deeds.

When I started this guidance-directed technology project, I didn't set out with such lofty goals as trying to change the world. Yet I would clearly change my own world. I wanted to better understand it, perhaps get some answers to those mysterious life questions we all seek, such as: What is the nature of the universe, and What part do I play in it?

I wasn't a scientist, physicist, or engineer, so I was starting out with only a rudimentary knowledge of the physical sciences. Even today, I understand more than I can explain in technical terms. I gladly leave those explanations to those who can better articulate such complex subjects. Climbing the academic ladder and getting a doctorate may provide you with a degree of respectability and acceptability, but I quickly learned that I knew even less than I thought in the greater scheme of things. I was being sent back to school to start with the basics.

Chapter 8
WHAT'S AN ALGORITHM?

"If I were again beginning my studies, I would follow the advice of Plato and start with mathematics."– GALILEO

My first lesson was pretty straightforward. My Guides informed me that if I was to know my world, I had to first understand the language of math. Upon hearing this news, I immediately knew I was in serious trouble. Math was my worst subject in school. Up until high school, I was an above average student. That changed when I went from simple math to the introduction of algebra, geometry, and calculus. This higher form of math was like a foreign language to me. It was abstract, and I couldn't see how it related to the real world. Maybe I just had a lousy teacher, but nevertheless I eked by with nothing higher than average grades in these subjects. My brain didn't seem to be wired for this kind of logic. Conceptually, it didn't make sense to me and caused me to feel somewhat stupid. I didn't understand why I couldn't grasp it as easily as others and avoided anything math-related after high school like the plague. I accepted the fact that, for some reason, I was missing this higher math gene and was simply "math challenged." Besides I had other talents, I rationalized. No one can be good at everything.

I dreaded taking the Graduate Records Exam (GRE), which I needed to pass in order to get into a Master's Program in Psychology. The exam tested for math proficiency among other things. Preparing for it, I bought a book that explained math formulas to help solve questions asked on the test. I panicked as I paged through the book. The explanations were even harder to understand. It was clear I needed another book just to understand the study guide! Every time I tried to study it, forcing myself to learn what I needed to know, I would fall asleep. My brain would just shut down and have none of it. Consequently, I ended up guessing most of the math questions on the GRE test. All I could do was hope and pray for the best.

I can't say I was surprised when I got my results back and my math scores were abysmal. But since I had done so well on the other sections of the test, thankfully, it balanced out my overall score and I passed. I rationalized away the whole experience by telling myself: "I do not need to be a math wizard to do good psychotherapy."

So I thought I had put this whole math thing behind me, until I was informed by my new Guides that I had signed on for a project that was, believe it or not, all about math. Was this some kind of cosmic joke? I had told clients for years that when you run from something, it has a tendency to pursue you: What you resist, often persists. With this project, I had come full circle back to my fear of math.

I couldn't help but wonder why a real mathematician hadn't been sought out who already understood all these concepts. Certainly that made more sense. Who were these Guides that were now asking me to face my self-perceived limitations and fears? I learned that they are multi-dimensional light beings, dedicated to helping man during great times of evolutionary crisis. They refer to themselves as part of the original "Found-ers" of our race (more on this in Chapter 14, The Founders).

I also learned that one of the reasons I was a part of this pro-ject was because I *was*, in essence, a math dummy. (They obvi-ously didn't use those disparaging words, but I got the gist.) The rationale was that, since I did not come in with any preconceived notions of existing theoretical math principles, I would be unlikely to over-analyze to distraction the information I would be given. I didn't know enough about math to say, "Well, that won't work," thereby slowing down the development process. What they wanted was a fresh mind to learn a whole new way of mathematical thinking. Sometimes life gives you your greatest gifts disguised as nightmares. I know that now. I certainly didn't back then.

What they began showing me was that everything that exists in our universe has a unique mathematical signature. Every number encompasses vibrational energies that affect all matter. In essence, EVERYTHING is about math and math affects EVERYTHING—even our DNA, which is the blueprint of creation.

DNA is our internal programming software. It's like a bio-logical Internet that stores all kinds of information. It dictates our genetic heritage and determines how we age. Yet, I knew very little about DNA, most of it culled from criminal trials and TV dramas. I found myself flashing back to the tagline of the TV show NUMB3RS: *"Using numbers, we can solve the biggest mysteries we know."*

It wasn't until April 2003 (a month before my near-death ex-perience) that the Human Genome Project declared they had completed the final sequencing of the human genome after more than a decade of work. In July of that same year, at the Genetic Congress in Melbourne, Australia, the world's leading geneticists began to realize they had missed the bigger picture.

I was astounded to learn that after all their work, we still only understand less than five percent of our DNA. The other 95%, still remains shrouded in mystery. When scientists explored human genes, the powerhouse of the genome, they identified specific sections of the gene, which they called "coding regions." These coding regions are packed with instructions for building proteins, which are the building blocks of life. Proteins form the structural components of our hair, skin, hormones, enzymes that digest food, and energy metabolism. They also found regions in the genes that were non-coded—meaning they did not encode for protein sequencing or regulation. Because scientists didn't understand the function of these non-coded regions, they assumed it had no relevance and labeled it "Junk DNA." This is the 95% we haven't figured out—which is pretty much all of it. Dismissing it as meaningless is akin to doing only 5% of your homework studies and then expecting you know enough to start teaching the class.

Science has come a little further since 2003. They now postulate that this "Junk DNA" is somehow involved in the evolution of new genes and possibly gene repair, but no one is certain. "Evolution" is the key word here, but not in the way they might assume. I was shown that these non-coded regions are extremely important because this is where man's true evolutionary programming lies. Yes, the key to man is hidden within man. But it's all about timing. It can't be opened until its ready to be unlocked. You could say that everything in the universe is subject to change, and everything is right on schedule. And it appears man's evolutionary growth switch is being triggered right now--at this very point in time.

It starts with an increased awareness to see more clearly through the lies and deceit and recognize the substance of truth. It's not happening to everyone all at once. It never does. The unaware are still unaware that they are unaware. But they, too, will eventually get there. And it serves to connect us with our divine heritage and open each and every one of us to our true soul potential. I'm not talking about man-made riches and wealth or prestige, but an intrinsic ability to see how we are all connected to each other and we are all in this together like some grand spiritual science project.

I was surprised to discover that even our DNA is mathematically coded and in order to speak to it, we need to speak to it in a language it understands--which is math. DNA is our internal programming software. It's our biological Internet. It has its own internal mechanism, which responds to certain algorithmic coding. This ultimately led me to learning about the nature of "algorithms."

What's an algorithm? It's a step-by-step procedure for solving a mathematical problem. If you assemble a set of numbers (information) together, where each number's vibration affects matter differently, they can then be combined synergistically to create a desired result (or solve the problem). That's the complex definition. More simply, algorithms are used extensively in computer software to make a program run. They're even used in cooking. A recipe for baking cookies is an algorithm. Basically, they are a set of instructions to follow to get a specific desired outcome.

What I was being shown was that our DNA not only reacts to human language, but it most definitely responds to mathematical information or "algorithms" giving it instructions. This was knowledge already existed long ago. In fact, the "new science" of quantum physics is really the "old wisdom" of our ancestors-- sometimes known as "metaphysics." I was directed to go back to the Pythagorean sciences of vibrational energies, which had been handed down from Ancient Egyptian times. The Pythagoreans really knew and understood this stuff.

I went back and took a closer look at the Ancient Greeks. Pythagoras was born in 580 B.C. and taught that reality is essentially mathematical in nature. He believed that a system of principles existed behind numbers. In the 6th Century, Pythagoreans reduced everything to a number. Numbers were conceived as the principle and innermost essence of the various manifestations of Universal Mind. They were related to vibrational states that affect the energy field. Pythagoras claimed he learned this from the Ancient Egyptians. Numbers were symbols for alchemy, power, and the very essence of nature.

The Egyptian Creation Myth hints at this: "I am One that transforms into Two; I am Two that transforms into Four; I am Four that transforms into Eight. After this I am ONE again." This myth might be better understood if we take into consideration that the Egyptians knew the periodic table of elements is formed of groups repeating in patterns of eight. Even the doubling of the human cell proceeds in eight stages. They encapsulated this in the infinity symbol, meaning "Life Regeneration."

Like Pythagoras had with the Ancient Egyptians, I was shown strange symbols that I had never seen before which contained information that could not be translated into English language terms. They were universal in nature, yet these symbols resonated with information and, grouped together, gave instructions. Our brains are not wired to see visual reality as numbers. We don't see flowers as numbers or stones as numbers, yet on a different level of perceptual reality this exists. In our world, we would classify this as a brain disorder and call it one of the many manifestations of "synesthesia." I learned that the inventor Nikola Tesla had a number form of synesthesia and was fixated on threes. Perhaps this contributed to his visionary genius of being able to see the world's hidden mysteries better than others.

I thought about how numbers were the only constant—a universal language that could span all worlds and species. When we send time capsules into space, hoping to reach some far off galaxy or race, what form do we send it in? We send it in numbers, formulas and/or equations that are universally consistent and therefore recognizable. The contents of the *Voyager Golden Record* that was launched into space in 1977 aboard Voyager 1, included what we understood about the mathematical and physical quantities of Earth, the Solar System, its planets, our DNA, and chemical compositions that encompass life here. Numbers can be a great way of reading a civilization's reality and seeing how far they have evolved in terms of universal knowledge.

My own world was now filled with numbers and images. I would be directed to images on the Internet when my Guides could not find any known conceptual reference in my own internal memory banks. There was power in naming what was desired, such as "Self-Love," and I would be given multiple symbols or images that embodied that vibration as well as the numbers with which they resonated. This was a fascinating behind-the-scenes look at the beginnings of the art of alchemy formulation. But this formulation was just a preliminary step, before it became an algorithm.

There were days when I would just sit in an altered-like state and be given sets and series of numbers, which I wrote down for hundreds of different properties. They became "the Codes." I had already started with a list of basic programs, so it was a matter of working down my list and seeing what my Guides thought was necessary to include within each program. They were soon directing me to add more spiritually-based versus physically-oriented programs. I thought I was creating an anti-aging device. My Guides clearly had other plans.

Behind each individual program, such as Energy Boost, might be 50-100 different coded algorithms. By the time I would finish with all the coding there would be well over 5,000 different algorithms. No program was ever alike. Numbers were given for basic elements, solids, liquids, herbs, minerals, vitamins, even emotions before being translated to binary code (0+1) sequencing, which is the language of computers. It became complicated, and it all sounded beyond anything I had ever done.

It took almost a year, in what would turn out to be a five-year developmental process, to bring forth--or in essence, channel--

the coded information I was given. Sometimes my Guides would show me strange symbols which looked like some other planetary language, or I would be shown ancient hieroglyphics that they wanted encoded into the technology. Our DNA would understand it and use it if it was needed, I was told. I was being reassured that the language of our DNA, our internal biological software, was indeed binary sequencing.

In many ways it made sense, even from my limited mathematical perspective. We are currently in the Age of Information. It's no coincidence that in the last 20 years we have had an explosion in technology—much of it in computer programming. These ideas and thoughts were seeded down in order to serve an important function. The intelligence behind this acceleration is intended to help the human race quickly link to its living WHOLE to expand its connected awareness. We are moving from collective "unconsciousness" to collective "consciousness." This awakening is the key step in our evolutionary process. And once the awakening begins there is no turning back, no closing the door or pretending to live in a bubble. The device my Guides asked me to help create was only another link in that process, and there would be more coming down the pike. An old way is dying, and a new transition or beginning is now on the horizon.

Everything has sped up. It's not our imagination. Events are happening faster and more profoundly. Many are and have been manifesting their greatest fears, while others are making 180° changes in their lives, careers, personal and family relationships. On all levels, we are clearing out the old and preparing for something new, whether we are consciously aware of it or not. Even back then, I had noticed how much more difficult my clients' presenting problems were than ever before. I observed more people either getting chronically ill or checking out of the planet because the energy acceleration for some was becoming too difficult to comfortably navigate. To fight the ongoing changes only seems to make the situation more challenging. All organisms on the planet and the Earth itself are subject to this change: global warming, extreme weather patterns, increased seismic and solar flare activity. The signs of change are everywhere, both in nature and man. This should not be taken as a sign of doom and gloom. Death always precedes rebirth—clearing out the old and making way for new life. It is a positive sign.

Technological change was quickly going through its own rebirth, as was I. Coming from an EEG neurofeedback background, I was used to thinking in terms of frequency. Rife worked with healing frequencies, as did other energetic devices on the market. What I was shown was evolving beyond that. I became aware of the subtle energy differences between frequencies and mathematical information. Frequencies, or a unit of frequency known as a "Hertz" (Hz, after its discoverer Heinrich Hertz), are measured in cycles per second. It's a standard measurement.

However, number-based information or algorithms are different. They are "non-Hertzian" in nature. Unlike Hertzian wave frequencies, they reside in the realm of what is known as "subtle energy." This non-Hertzian energy is being proposed as a "higher dimensional energy" consisting of pure information patterns, which mediate communication between all cells in the body. This higher dimensional energy is believed to be associated with health and the natural healing process.

Traditional medicine has mostly discounted energy medicine due to lack of acceptable and replicable testing methodology. The problem for researchers is that this energy that pervades our universe cannot be measured using conventional, Newtonian physics testing methods. Consequently, quantum physicists have been scrambling to find new testing methodology to validate their work, and this takes time. They have to think outside the box as the world moves into the quantum pond. The concept of even energetically clearing a lab between subtle energy experiments may seem Merlinesque to many Newtonian physicists. Scientists can be rather stubborn and resistant to change until there is irrefutable proof in front of their eyes, and even then they may still dismiss the evidence. However, with the world changing so rapidly, the learning curve can be painful when they are challenged to throw out existing beliefs for new information coming in at such a rapid speed. Whether they are willing to accept it or not, subtle energy is only the tip of the iceberg.

Beyond subtle energy is an even higher dimensional level, called the spiritual energy level that quantum physicists such as David Bohm first wrote about in 1952. Disruption in the subtle energy field leads to disease in the physical body. This means that, to adequately address disease, you have to go beyond the physical body to the very consciousness of the cells in the energy body. We can change the consciousness of the cells, but again we need to speak to it in a language it understands—mathematics. How can mathematical algorithms accomplish such a task? I quickly discovered it was only one component of a multi-tiered equation.

Chapter 9
FRACTALS OF GOD

"God used beautiful mathematics in creating the world."
– PAUL DIRAC

I began to see possible answers to some of my more profound questions in the world of hidden numbers, like some great DaVinci Code I was tasked with solving. I was fascinated and quite in awe of the concept that even my vitamins had their own unique mathematical signature. I fantasized that if I fed that mathematical information to the body, might it mean I didn't have to take a vitamin ever again? At that time, I had no definitive or empirical answers to such questions. But it certainly intrigued me. I was reminded of the American Humorist, Dorothy Parker, who said: *"The cure for boredom is curiosity. There is no cure for curiosity."* And my curiosity was insatiable.

It wasn't just numbers, but patterns of numbers that I could see all around me. I had never paid much attention to such things before. And like so many of us, where there is lack of awareness, there is lack of understanding and meaning. The best mysteries are always hidden in plain sight. We overlook the obvious all the time. If it's too simple, we oftentimes dismiss it.

If you observe your every-day environment, you'll see there are simple sequencing patterns that resonate in all of nature. The harmonics of all living organisms are governed by a principle called the Golden Ratio or Phi. Phi is a number with no mathematical solution. The decimals just keep on going into infinity without ever repeating themselves. Its proportional geometry is seen in the growth patterns of plants, trees, leaves, nautilus shells, snowflakes, clouds, even the bones of the human hand. It can be found everywhere in art, music, design, flowers, facial symmetry, and even in the stock market. Leonardo DaVinci referred to its use in his painting of "The Last Supper" as the Divine Proportion. Everything in the universe is based on this proportion: 1 to 1.618. Plato went so far as to call the Phi Ratio (1.618) *the key to the physics of the cosmos.* You can't help but ask, "Is God a Mathematician?"

The ancients too referred to these principles as "sacred geometry" and incorporated them into their most revered monuments. The Egyptians used sacred geometry in the Great Pyramids, the Greeks in the Parthenon, and later these same principles could even be seen in the Gothic temples. Modern day architects incorporate sacred geometry in buildings to balance the environment and to help create a healthy vibrational place to work and live and resonate (known as bio-architecture).

The ancients believed that spirals based on Phi called "Golden Mean Spirals" measured the Creative Forces. They were seen as the most powerful symbols for transformation, regeneration, and accelerated cellular healing. The mystics of that time taught that it opened a doorway into no time and space (meaning an inter-dimensional wormhole) and influenced not only the physical body, but the spiritual, emotional, and mental body as well. For them, the Golden Mean Spiral represented the Christ Consciousness grid of the entire human race. It comes as no surprise then that human DNA exhibits these spiral strands.

I kept seeing these colorful spiral images in my mind. They swirled and pulsed as if they were living, breathing organisms. They had an energy all their own, and my Guides were clearly telling me to pay close attention to their significance. This was my first introduction to the field of "fractals." I had never heard about fractals, and certainly I had never seen an animated, moving one. When I finally did, I knew with all certainly that there was some kind of powerful life force behind these geometrical patterns.

The modern-day mathematician, Benoit Mandelbrot, was the first to develop a "theory of roughness" in nature (phenomenon in the real world) and the field of fractal geometry to help prove it. Mandelbrot coined the term "fractal" in 1975 and was also one of the first to use computer graphics to create fractal geometric repetitive patterns from simple mathematical rules. In 1979, he discovered what became known as the famous "Mandelbrot Set," which was credited as "the most astonishing discovery in the entire history of mathematics" by science-fiction writer Arthur C. Clarke.

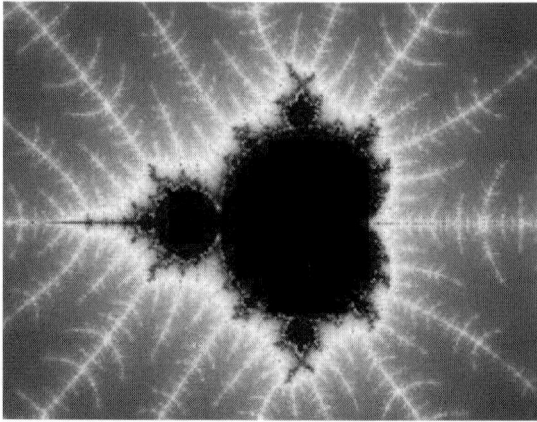

Mandelbrot's famous "Julia Set"

Although Mandelbrot coined the term "fractal," he believed it was not a science he invented. He believed he merely re-discovered its significance. Fractals are created using simple mathematical equations, which are then fed back into the equation creating similar patterns that repeat in an infinite feedback loop. Fractals are like those Russian Matryoshka dolls—a doll within a doll within a doll to infinity. If you zoomed into any one part of a fractal you would see the entirety of its whole like a hologram, but with slight differences. We may live in a world of finite boundaries, but within each organism, whether it is human, plant, mineral, or animal, lies an infinity of information levels. If we looked inside the human body, our bronchial tree and blood vessels look fractal. An entire universe exists within every one of us and outside of us, suggesting we live in a fractal universe, as I'm sure Mandelbrot realized. But—my favorite question again-- what does it all mean?

Everything in nature is fractal and so is consciousness. If you have one thought over and over again, you are fractalizing that thought and giving it more energy. Repeating patterns of thought make it more meaningful and give it power, substance, and form. "Be careful what you dwell on" has a basis in the science of fractals. Some call it the Law of Attraction—what you dwell upon you draw to you, but behind it all is the science of fractacality, and it's quickly becoming the new science of life.

This got me thinking: If we live in a fractal universe, is God fractal and are we all fractals of God? If we were made in the "image and likeness" of God as religions tell us, are we not all God-like as well, within God's universe? Some people may recoil at the thought of calling themselves or others Gods, but in our true essence we ARE fractals of God. We all come from the Source, the Whole—known as GOD. We are divine god-like beings and souls having a human experience. We may screw up while having that human experience, but is that not part of the growth and expansion of all the parts of the Whole in a quest to learn and evolve? We are all connected in this fractal body of God. Some will get caught in the illusion of wealth, power, and fame, but even in their disconnectedness, they are still connected to the fractal Source. Our evolution is also fractal. As a race, we are perpetually repeating old patterns in a continuous feedback loop, whether they are setbacks or advancements. Whether we know it or not, we are all playing our part in each other's evolutionary growth. So, ultimately, fractals underlie the very structure of life.

I saw visions that at one time we were all part of one great big energy source. The Big Bang Theory may have some basis in fractal science. This energy Source, or unified Godhead, expanded and contracted much like when a new galaxy or star system is born. Everything that emerged from this Source was pure energy. Anything that was ultimately created out of it such as humans, animals, plants, etc., was also matter made up of energy. We are all slightly different, but still we are all energy from the Source. All parts contain the energy of the Whole. The concept that we are all fractals of God opens up a totally new understanding of the mysteries of the universe. We each came to be on this Earth to have the experience of creating and manifesting our soul's desires. We are all learning something different, and whether we know it or not, each of our experiences, good or bad, contributes to the knowledge of the Whole. While we are soul spirits having a human experience together, ultimately our final goal is to return to the fractal Source to share this divine experience.

My Guides encouraged me to explore these concepts of Source and Light in conjunction with what I was learning to create. I needed to understand how all parts contributed to the whole of this project, and fractals were a part of that whole. I was shown that placing a person in a fractal field brings about an intensification of life force electrical charge which contributes to phase conjugation or a state of coherence. In other words, where there is true coherence, there is divine ONENESS.

Was it then possible for fractal patterns to help restore health? Perhaps a strong healthy body's fractal patterns are intact, and an unhealthy one has disrupted patterns. Like plants that have lost their vitality, they also seem to lose their fractal patterns. Their growth is slow and erratic. I noticed this in a coral tree near my house, which had been struggling to survive for many years. The limb growth was chaotic and very few leaves ever grew on its branches, unlike the other healthy coral trees nearby. Still, this tree managed to stay alive, but just barely. I tried to direct healing energy to the tree, without much success. One day, I walked around the tree, allowed it to speak to me, and I felt a strong drowning sensation. I looked around, spotted a water main shut off pipe station about 30 feet away, and I knew that there was an underground leak somewhere that flooded and consequently overwhelmed the tree's life force. Although it might have been too late to save such a tree (since the city had already made plans to cut it down), its erratic growth patterns really caught my attention. It was like a fractal field collapsing in upon itself. It fascinated me. How had I never recognized this before? I asked my Guides whether the use of fractals could ultimately help in the restoration of health.

Yes, but the key to achieving this fractal amplification process was coupling it with the mathematical algorithms they had given me. This would strengthen the information Codes coming through the fractal field, giving them instruction for greater amplification. To do so, I had to first create the swirling fractals that would carry along the Codes--not enmeshed inside the fractals, but with the ability to run alongside the Codes in a oneness/coherent relationship. They eventually led me to someone who not only had that ability, but had also spent years of his life devoted to fractal creation. It was as if we had just been waiting to meet up at this destiny point in time and, as fate would have it, he lived within 50 miles of me.

All the parts were coming together, yet I still had to find someone I could trust to put it into a software program. I didn't have the time to start learning complex software programming, which could take years to learn and get up to speed on, so I started putting out feelers in the tech community. I wanted a master programmer, someone with lots of experience working on cutting-edge projects that were out of the norm, someone who could think outside the box. I needed to be able to work well with the person and vice versa. My Guides already had someone in mind and, through a roundabout way, we finally connected. He didn't have a background in energy devices and didn't know much about the energetic or spiritual world in general; but he was a master at programming, and we resonated well together. Whereas my Guides had not much cared for the energy of the first two inventors I'd tried to work with, they let me know I could trust this person. He had integrity. He had no idea where my information came from. In fact, he worried for me that what I wanted to do might be crazy enough to leave me penniless but, like my father, he never voiced it. It would be years later that I learned the true extent of his concerns. Back then, I had doubts too, so I totally understood where he was coming from. This would be a journey for both of us. On a higher level, he had already made a contract to help me bring forth this project.

Despite having a great programmer to work with, my doubts were always in the background, rearing their ugly head every now and then--especially whenever I encountered another setback. New pictures in the puzzle of this project continued to emerge. Every step of my journey was entangled with a lesson in science, the universe—and ultimately the ability to trust. Every question I got answers to only raised countless more new questions.

It was a good thing that these new Guides of mine had not shown me the full scope of this project up front. I know now that complex software development can be the fastest route to insanity. It's like playing a master chess game, where you are forever trying to figure out all the moves and possible outcomes in advance, but on several levels simultaneously. It's complicated, and I knew I had made the right decision in finding someone extremely competent. As a result of my own experience, I have great empathy and respect for all software developers.

I think of the Internet as another fractal manifestation of Source. Here many minds, unhampered by time and distance, can instantaneously communicate, sharing information and experiences to learn and grow from. The Internet has been one of the key instruments to increase awareness as well as make it more difficult for those trying to practice deceit in the world at large. While this is the Age of Information, it is also the Age of Universal Truth. And, in the quest for truth comes heightened awareness and ultimately, human evolution.

Kathy J. Forti, Ph.D.

Chapter 10
SOUND AS HEALING

"Do you know that our soul is composed of harmony?"
– LEONARDO DA VINCI

From the start I knew sound was a key component of this technology project. I was shown that the universe was brought into existence out of sound. The universe vibrates with energy from the Source and, without vibration, there is no sound. Sound waves come from vibrations. They say the first sense to develop in utero is sound. Infants react to their mother's voice and to loud noises--especially music. When a person dies, the last sense to go is their hearing. Sound affects all of us. Even those who are deaf feel sound vibrations with their entire body.

Years earlier, I had my own experience with using sound for healing. In 1982, I was living in a small town in Kansas, having a dark night of my soul. I moved there directly from New York City and consequently experienced culture shock. I hooked up with that young psychologist I had had the astral experience with at the Monroe Institute, and the lack of mental stimulation in a small town drove me crazy. I felt like I was suffocating and my life was passing me by. Since there were no external distractions (like in New York City), I was forced to go inward and face my inner fears, vulnerabilities, and perceived self-limitations. Not something any of us look forward to doing. I had no idea where I was going in my life. I lived in a town where I had no friends, nor could I find work in the journalism news business. I felt considerable anxiety. I had to take jobs I was extremely over-qualified for, turning it into a lesson in humility. I worked part time in the town's country club office doing secretarial work by day, and I was a cocktail waitress in a country western bar at night until 2:00 a.m. It was a packed hot spot in town, with two-stepping cowboys who got into fights in the parking lot and carried gun racks on their amped-up pickup trucks. The town had more churches and bars than any town should have. I felt like I had been dropped into redneck heaven, and I rationalized away each night at work telling myself I was just "doing social research" for a book I would write someday. While my psychologist boyfriend helped the anguished by day, I was mentally falling apart at night. But, even from nightmares comes learning. In Kansas, the Land of Oz, I learned about self-healing.

There was a roller skating rink in that little Kansas town, where I loved to skate. My great uncle had once owned a small skating rink in Chicago, and my father and his sister, my Aunt Jo, had been rink guards growing up. I learned to skate from watching them. Skating symbology even invaded my dream states. When I was on the right track, I would see myself skating and dancing along without obstacles, having a good time. When I was off my life path and making poor choices, I would see myself in my dreams having to take off my skates and I'd go nowhere. I soon recognized the dream signs.

What happened in this particular Kansas skating rink was no dream—but you could call it a wake-up call. On one especially crowded night at the roller rink, I was skating backwards when someone on my tail fell right behind me. There was nowhere to go but down if I didn't want to cause a pile up. My left hand went down to break my fall and it hit pretty hard. I have a very high tolerance to pain, so not until later in the evening, when it began really swelling and the pain intensified, did I realize it was more than bruised. It was after midnight, and we had out-of-town guests staying over. I didn't want to wake them, so I got up and drove myself to the emergency room in the early morning hours. They x-rayed it, told me I had broken a very difficult bone to heal, and slapped a cast on my arm. I had never broken anything before. I thought all bones took about six weeks to heal, and I figured I could live with that. Unfortunately, I was then informed by the orthopedic surgeon on call that the navicular bone, also known as a scaphoid displaced fracture between the thumb and forefinger, oftentimes requires surgery and can take 3-6 months to heal due to atrophy. He also talked about the possibility of my requiring physical therapy due to the nature of these particular types of bone breaks. The thought of having a cast on my arm for half a year, and possibly surgery, horrified me. It would mean missing out on a canoeing trip I planned in two months. It was summer time, and I thought of all the things I would miss out on. The only positive note was that it happened to my left hand, and I was right-hand dominant.

I grieved for my fallen hand for about a day, then decided to take action. I was determined to heal my bone in record time and go on that canoe trip. I had already seen evidence of the power of intention while working at the New York City Ronald McDonald House two years earlier. Dr. Elisabeth Kübler-Ross, one of the greatest teachers on death and dying, who is now deceased, had come to visit the children while I was there, and she talked about using positive visualization to help combat their cancer. One little girl with long beautiful hair, who was to start receiving chemotherapy for retina blastoma, told everyone emphatically that she was not going to have her hair fall out like everyone else who received chemo. She had clearly set her mind to making this happen and visualized it. And the miracle of it was that she didn't lose her hair like all the others. I thought I would also try visualization on my injured hand, but decided to add a few twists of my own into the mix.

I asked my physician if I could get a copy of my x-ray and, of course, I told him I would pay for the extra cost. From his suspicious reaction, it must have been a first time request. He wanted to know why and what for. I don't remember what I told him, since I wasn't sure myself at the time. To his credit, he got me a copy and immediately I took typewriter whiteout fluid and went over the crack in the bone on the x-ray so that it looked whole and completely healed. I put it up on my bathroom mirror so that I would always see it whole every time I looked at it.

Going on instinct alone, I decided sound would help heal my bone. This was back in the early '80s, before sound research had even supported such an outlandish theory. So I picked the most inspirational music I could find at the time, which was Vangelis' *Chariots of Fire* album. I'm not a runner, but if it made even me want to run when I played it, I figured it was probably a good choice. Back then, everyone had big stereo floor speakers, and I wanted to really feel the music. I placed one of the big speakers flat on the floor and sat down beside it. I laid my arm with the cast atop it. That's when a really crazy idea popped into my head, and I went to look for and found a piece of quartz crystal someone had given me. I put it in the hand with the cast, and then put my arm back on the stereo speaker. I played the Vangelis music and visualized my hand already healed and doing all these amazing things—climbing mountains, swimming through oceans, and it became a beacon of light leading me on. I visualized with the music—in essence re-programming my body to believe it was already whole, thereby speeding up the healing process. I could feel the sound vibrations coming up through the speaker into my arm, and with it came shooting sensations of heat and pulsing. I wasn't sure what was happening, but I knew it was important that I continue to do it one to two times a day for at least 20-30 minutes. I also knew inherently that I had to be careful how I talked about the injury. It's always so tempting with friends to go into our story spiel about how it happened and what the doctor said, and all the misery involved and "poor me." When friends asked about when the cast was coming off, I would always say, "Any day now." I was intent on erasing the three to six month prognosis from my internal data banks.

After four weeks of doing my unorthodox healing ritual, I had to go back to the doctor for new x-rays. He removed the cast, took new x-rays, and disappeared to review them. He came back into the room looking very perplexed. "It's healed, isn't it?" I blurted out. He hesitated, thinking what to say before frowning. "Well, it looks surprisingly good for four weeks. But I know these bones. They don't heal that fast." And with that he slapped another cast back on my arm and sent me on my way.

I was devastated at first, but I refused to dwell on it, and went back to my Vangelis healing ritual. A week later, I started having dreams that my hand was already healed, so I went to the hardware store. Bucking the medical profession, something I had never done before, I decided I would take off the cast myself. I am not advising others do this, but the sheer certainty of what I was doing gave me the courage to follow through.

I had no idea what kind of instrument would cut through a plaster cast. I walked down the hardware store aisles trying out different tools. I quickly eliminated small saws as an option and focused on heavy-duty pruning shears instead. It is quite challenging to safely cut through a cast. It's almost impossible to make a straight cut due to leverage, but I knew it would not be an easy task.

I made my purchase, and it took over an hour to free my arm once I set myself to the task back at home. My hand was all white and wrinkled with dead skin when I unveiled it. I washed it several times and immediately started using a small hand exercise ball to increase muscle strength. One day later, my hand felt completely back to normal. No twinges, pain, swelling, or weakness. It took just a little over five weeks to heal my hand, which amazed even me. I never returned to the doctor, and every time I hear the *Chariots of Fire* music my hand seems to pulse with energy. I'm sure it's due to cellular memory of the healing.

Years later, I would learn that they had used sound to help re-generate frogs' legs. So when I became entrenched with this new project, I already knew that sound was a key component, and my Guides didn't have to convince me. What was different this time was that I was being shown which sounds to pursue and why.

Sound is a bridge between the unconscious and the conscious world. It speaks to us on many levels and can evoke feelings of love, fear, bliss, agitation, and a myriad of other emotions. Indeed, the quickest way to enter the energy field is through sound frequencies and our ancient brethren knew this and used it. Centuries ago, certain sound frequencies were used in the Gothic churches and incorporated into the sacred Gregorian chants. They were called Solfeggio frequencies, and these tones brought about a resonance in the body that had strong healing and transformational properties. Somehow, these special tones were presumably lost by the Catholic Church centuries ago. They were rediscovered by naturopathic physician Dr. Joseph Puleo after being led to them as a result of a mystical experience. There were six original tones, which were later expanded to nine in three sets. The frequencies are listed below. When added together both horizontally and/or vertically they can be reduced to a single number of 3, 6, or 9:

396 – the number 9 (3+9+6=18, 1+8=9)
639
963

174 – the number 3 (1+7+4=12, 1+2 = 3)
417
741

285 – the number 6 (2+8+5=15, 1+5=6)
528
852

This kind of reminds one of a Sudoku puzzle. But what does it mean? One clue comes from the famous visionary and the greatest inventor our world has ever known--Nikola Tesla. Tesla said: *"If you only knew the magnificence of the numbers 3, 6, and 9, you would have the keys to the universe."* He believed that somehow these numbers served as portals to other dimensions and expanded consciousness.

My quest led me to the Fibonacci number sequencing, which is a close cousin to Phi. Fibonacci sequencing maps out natural growth patterns in nature (e.g., tree branching, artichoke flowering, rabbit growth population, etc.). Each subsequent number is the sum of the previous two. The sequence usually starts with 0 and 1, but I discovered if we start the Fibonacci sequence with 0+3, 3, 6, 9, 15, 24, 39, 63, 102, 165, 267, 432, etc., each of those numbers when reduced to a single digit also comes out to 3, 6, and 9.

For most of my adult life, I have suspected that certain hit songs become big hits as a direct result of the use of certain universal overtones that resonate harmonically on a molecular level. The cellular body recognizes them due to their mathematical resonance. Each of the original six Solfeggio tones was intended to be music to the soul or "secret ear" and is believed to address certain areas of the human condition. They were believed to be the six tones used to bring forth the atomic structure of the universe during the six days of creation. They are also believed to be the keys to portals to other dimensions. Below are the frequency tones and their healing effect upon the emotional, physical, and spiritual body:

396 Hz – Liberating Guilt and Fear

417 Hz – Undoing Situations and Facilitating Change

528 Hz – Transformation and Miracles (Genetic biochemists use this frequency to repair broken DNA)

639 Hz – Connecting Relationships

741 Hz – Awakening Intuition

852 Hz – Returning to Spiritual Order

These ancient Solfeggio tones stimulate healing potential because they serve to retune and balance the body to a frequency of vibratory health. I learned that when these tones are coupled with the algorithmic Codes I was given, and played with fractals, they can be used synergistically as a powerful force for transformation and change. The pieces were all coming together. "All parts contribute to the Whole," I kept hearing. No one part alone has all the answers.

Kathy J. Forti, Ph.D.

Chapter 11
CRYSTAL TRANSMISSION

"Every particular in nature, a leaf, a drop, a crystal, a moment in time is related to the Whole and partakes of the perfection of the Whole."
— RALPH WALDO EMERSON

While I was getting pieces of the "Whole," and started putting all these layers together in a software program I could hopefully use on me, if no one else, I was mystified about how this information might be delivered to the body. Transmission was clearly a weak link until I started seeing visions in my head of Superman, the "Man of Steel." Needless to say, I thought that was extremely odd. Yet, my Guides kept fast forwarding to the scene in the movie from the Fortress of Solitude where Superman is in a cold Arctic cave downloading the history of his race through kryptonite "memory crystals" that stored thousands of terabytes by today's standards. Every time Superman picked up a crystal and held it in his hand, the picture in my mind froze and I would mentally zoom in. It was obvious they wanted me to examine something already familiar to my internal data banks, albeit even if it was only from a movie's generated special effects scene.

Transmission though crystals. I admitted it was an interesting concept. I instantly thought back to my roller skating accident, where I had instinctively used a small crystal in my hand to help in the healing process. I must have unconsciously known its potential even back then. Now, I needed to consciously learn why my Guides were so emphatic that quartz crystal be used.

I learned that crystals are living things. They are alive and respond to both physical and oral direction. For centuries, their beauty has captivated us, and we inherently sense their mystery as we stare into their depths. The crystal's structure is oftentimes described as "lattice" due to its repeating symmetrical patterns. It appears three dimensional with its multiple layers—like nature's sculpting alchemy. This lattice structure is the key to its power. It allows a crystal to store vast amounts of information and contributes to its electrical potential. When stress is placed across a crystal, it gives off a piezoelectric charge. It will vibrate and oscillate, creating a resonance or even a specific frequency. As I learned the properties of crystals, it occurred to me that I could find a way to stream the algorithms right into a crystal, thereby causing it to vibrate with the resonance of the codes.

To do this I needed double-terminated crystals. These crystals have faceted points at each end-- one end to take in the information and the other end to quickly release it to a person. Throughout the centuries, double-terminated quartz crystals have held a unique place in the realm of healing. The Native American shamans used double-terminated crystals in their healing rituals and ceremonies. The Greeks and Romans used them for divination and communicating with the Gods. Modern-day healers use them in psychic and spiritual ceremonies and claim they can help people at a distance to heal. Crystals appear to be very effective in amplifying positive thoughts and intentions.

Crystals also communicate with other crystals through a universal crystal matrix. If you put two similar crystals near each other, they will begin resonating in sync with the same information. They work in unison, amplifying the communication between the physical and an inter-dimensional spiritual realm. Distance is no obstacle--they work through some kind of quantum string theory network that sets up a crystal matrix grid much like our Internet. Ancient healers and mystics specifically chose quartz crystals because they knew their beauty and capabilities over other gems. They may not have known their modern-day, internet-like capabilities, but they clearly suspected crystals could do amazing things.

Once I started to understand crystals, it made perfect sense to me that I use them as transmission vehicles. But that still didn't explain how to attach them to a computer. My Guides showed me pictures of the particular type and look of crystals I needed. They were pure quartz crystals, rod-like in appearance, and they looked as clear as glass. I had never seen crystals this clear in any gem shop. I scoured the Internet looking for such things and came up empty-handed. Eventually, I learned quartz crystals could be lab grown--an expensive and timely process. It took me months of searching to find a lab in the world that could grow the size and specifications of crystals I was told I needed. I learned it takes a little over a month to grow each crystal using a hydrothermal method. They start by putting seed crystals in a pressured container called an autoclave and slowly adding silicon dioxide to control for clarity as it grows.

Flawless clarity seemed to be extremely important for how these crystals would be expected to perform. I knew that almost every electronic device used some type of silicon crystal chip that functioned as a semiconductor to carry out certain circuitry functions. They acted as oscillators for clocks. Data crystal chips have the ability to store, amplify, and transfer sensitive information. Once again, I thought back to how I had used vibratory sound with that small crystal in my hand to heal it after the skating accident. It served to amplify both my visualization and my healing intent.

Although the concept of crystal transmission may at first appear to many as "New Age" and possibly dismissible, I knew I was onto something uniquely different. This would be the first use of crystals attached to a computer, which also contains crystal components. Much later, I would learn that the Hadron Super Collider at the CERN particle physics laboratory in Meyrin, Switzerland, also uses crystals. Their Electromagnetic Photon Spectrometer (PHOS) is designed to measure the temperature of collisions by detecting the photons emerging from it. It's made up of over 60,000 rod-like crystals which are similar to what I was led to use. Science already knows the power of crystals. Crystals appear to be plugged into some collective field by which they have learned to communicate with other crystals. This is an information field that is not dependent on individual minds and appears to be outside of time and space.

Many scientists believe that a new energetic communication network may exist between cells in the body, much like quartz crystals. Dr. Vlail Kaznacheyev, the Director of the Institute for Clinical and Experimental Medicine in the Soviet Union, believes cells communicate through EMF (electromagnetic field) transmission. He used quartz crystals to successfully test this theory. In what is known as "the Kaznacheyev experiments," Kaznacheyev and his team measured the ability of two populations of cells, one diseased and one healthy, separated by a crystal barrier, and found they were able to communicate with each other. The EM field transmitted by the diseased cells was transmitted to the healthy cells, causing them to acquire the same diseased properties. When they repeated the same experiment with an ordinary glass window (not a crystal one), the healthy cells were not affected by the diseased cells. Crystals act as transmitters of information. If positive information could be actively transmitted to diseased cells via crystals, I began to imagine the possibilities.

Even the Ancient Egyptians seemed to be keyed into crystals. Interestingly, I learned that the King's Chamber in the Great Pyramid at Giza is the only chamber that is lined with hundreds of tons of silicone quartz crystal particles embedded into the granite beams. The particles are hexagonal and rhombohedral in shape. The rest of the pyramid is predominantly limestone, which has no conductive properties.

So why would the Ancient Egyptians have had the need for quartz properties in this mysterious chamber? Could the chamber and its unusually non-uniform shaped ceiling beams have been used for resonant tuning capabilities or to create a piezoelectric field? Interestingly enough, the properties of granite, which contain a high content of quartz, feldspar, and mica, are known to boost the flow of energy. Granite also allows sound to pass through it and quartz crystal is a transducer that transforms one form of energy into another.

Paul Horn, the musician that recorded the album *Inside the Great Pyramid*, discovered inside the King's Chamber that when he struck the sarcophagus coffer, the whole chamber resonated with the perfect frequency of 438 – the note A. He verified this using an electronic tuning device. The coffer had clearly been tuned to a specific frequency with the chamber becoming a resonator of that frequency and the quartz crystal in the walls played its role in that resonance. This brings up some pretty interesting questions. What were they really using the King's Chamber for?

The pyramids of Egypt were never intended for use as tombs—this is a widely believed misconception. Not one mummy has ever been found buried inside a pyramid. Some still espouse this belief, professing that grave robbers must have stolen the mummified bodies. This would be hard to pull off when many of those pyramids were sealed with undisturbed large granite stones for centuries. There are airshafts in the Great Pyramid, which have puzzled Egyptologists for centuries. If it was meant to be a sealed tomb to preserve mummification, then why the air vents, which would totally defeat that purpose? Airshafts signal it was needed for the people who would be working inside the pyramid who would need proper ventilation to breathe.

In the last 50 years, Egyptologists discovered that the airshaft in the King's Chamber is directly aligned with the Orion star constellation, specifically Orion's Belt, and the Queen's Chamber shaft is directly aligned to the Sirius star constellation. This is no coincidence. In fact, many of the sacred Ancient Egyptian temples are aligned with major stars in the Orion constellation. From the little known "Pyramid Texts," which were hieroglyphic writings taken off the walls of the chambers of the pyramid of Unas, we can surmise that the ancient Egyptians were involved in some kind of star transmission work. Could the use of crystals have been integral in their star-based religious ceremonies/rituals, which is why only the King's Chamber has heightened quartz properties? (More on this later.)

It seems apparent from the information I was given that quartz crystal is not just a pretty rock found in New Age gem shops. Crystal components, such as crystal semiconductor chips, can be found in every modern-day computer. Crystals have the ability to transfer information, generate a charge to power electronic devices, and who knows what else they might be capable of doing. One small crystal computer chip can be encoded with an unlimited amount of information in binary code. The more I learned about crystals, the more I resonated with the idea of lab-grown quartz crystal to transmit the algorithmic Codes.

Existing science shows that when you apply pressure or oscillation stress to a crystal, it generates heat and can give off a piezoelectric effect. I had already experienced this firsthand with the crystal healing experiment on my broken hand bone. I remember feeling that warm pulsing sensation shoot through my hand as it lay on the stereo speaker with a crystal clutched in my hand with the arm cast. At that time, I didn't know why this was, but I do remember being fascinated by the feeling of heat. It felt good. I felt plugged in, yet wasn't able to pinpoint the direct cause of the pulsing warmth.

I began to understand what had taken place. The human body is composed of millions of crystals, and the cells of our bodies are like liquid crystals. We are one big transmitting and receiving station, and working with crystals appears to amp up the energy field effect.

When my first order of double-terminated crystal rods arrived from the lab, they were stunningly beautiful. I held them in my hands and explored them from every angle. Pure quartz crystal is free of the impurities of trace elements, and I had never seen crystals so flawless that they looked like clear polished glass. This would make it easier to quickly stream the codes through the crystals, without storing the information. My Guides had stressed how important it was that the length be precise in size for resonance, and that the rods be four-sided to attune to Earth and pyramid energies. Four-sided, I was told, would be best for working with the body in the physical plane. Six-sided crystals would come later, for more spiritual work.

I pondered whether these lab-grown crystals would not only transmit information, but could they possibly take in the energy of other people's negative baggage when they were held? I read how people always advised clearing crystals either with salt water or bathing them in the sunlight to clear any negative energy they might have picked up from people, places, or things. This might prove to be a problem if many people used the same crystals. If the crystals were exposed to human diseased cells, like the Russian experiment, would they then transmit them to the next person using the crystal rods? It was a concern that proved unnecessary.

My Guides showed me that lab-grown crystals, due to their clarity, do not store negative energy. Since my crystals were double-terminated, they took in information, any information for that fact, and quickly released it. The information resonated through the crystal at one pointed end and rapidly released through the point at the other end to the person holding it. The crystals held onto the information only long enough to transmit it, meaning nanoseconds. This automatically made them self-cleaning in nature. They could be wiped down between users for hygiene purposes, but energetically, they would remain clean and clear.

My next concern was even more logistically perplexing. How was I to attach the crystals to the computer, which would stream the algorithm codes? This would require some type of signal converter. I consulted with an engineer who informed me that what I was trying to do was go from a digital signal to an analog one. The codes were binary (meaning digital) and the crystals were analog in nature. The human body, like crystals, apparently responds better to an analog signal than a digital signal.

While I was still contemplating how to connect the crystals to the Codes, I now had to think about manufacturing a digital-to-analog converter box. This is usually the stage where most people throw up their hands and say, Enough. It was getting more complicated with each new bit of information I received and certainly more costly. Where I had spent almost a year bringing forth the Codes, I now found that hardware was an even more daunting task. It was so far beyond my scope of knowledge. It sounded more like a guy's job than a woman's. That thought alone got my attention. It was a defeatist and sexist attitude. Who says a man could do this project any better than a woman? We defer to men too often to fix the electrical wiring, the plumbing, the car that's on the fritz, and our broken electronic equipment, because we know they like to tinker with such things and can usually get the job done. Women are not used to doing these things ourselves unless we have no other option. I had a flat tire once on the freeway on a very cold night, and no one would stop. It was the first time I learned how to change a tire myself. I figured it out, and I made it home in one piece. The lug nuts might have been a little looser than a man would have tightened them, but I did it. I knew I could learn to tackle this problem as well. It occurred to me that in the past, when I would be told I couldn't do something or it wasn't possible, it only served to make me more fixated on taking on the challenge.

Sometimes, you just need to walk away from something to get a fresh perspective. It was a nice sunny day so I decided to get my bicycle and go for a long ride. I live near the ocean in Santa Monica, California, and have always enjoyed riding along the oceanfront to clear my mind, be it winter or summer. As I rode along Venice Beach, I found myself continually staring down at my handlebars. I felt like my attention was purposely being directed to those black rubber grips.

All along, I had been trying to figure out some kind of square holder for my four-sided crystal rods, when it never occurred to me that square objects could also fit quite nicely into round holes—especially if the round hole receptacle has a gripping nature. A light bulb went off in my head. But of course—rubber holders! It was just the solution I was looking for. I bicycled home and immediately started calling rubber manufacturers. Eventually, I found one that didn't think my idea was crazy and agreed to work with me on a prototype. My crystals would have to be plugged into a signal converter box, which I knew meant the rubber holder had to be able to hold a cable jack and some kind of circuitry. I had to take a step back. I couldn't design the holder until I first knew what kind of signal box and cable jacks I needed.

This step actually happened faster than I thought. I found a company retiring their digital-to-analog converter box designs, due to lack of demand. There was more of a market for analog to digital, not digital to analog, which was my good fortune. I got them to send me a sample. Their sleek silver modern design reminded me of the design beauty of a Mac computer. I discarded the cables their converter box used and secured long six-foot cables of my own, after another exhaustive search for suppliers. I wanted those crystals cables to have the capability of reaching quite a distance. I then realized I needed to find circuits to insert into the rubber holders to hold the jacks. It was like being on a treasure hunt where each puzzle piece leads you to another piece you also need to find. I learned I needed to have those circuits soldered and find small copper wire springs to place around the circuit. This led to a copper wire company and another company to hand-solder each circuit individually so it could encircle one end of the double-terminated crystal. The algorithmic Codes needed to vibrate and oscillate the crystals to transmit the information that would stream through them.

During this entire process, I came across information that the Egyptians used copper tubes filled with crystals to aid in healing and connection to the Divine. They were called Rods of Ra and were used by priests and priestesses of the ancient Mystery School. It was time to bring the Rods of Ra into the 21st Century, using the latest computer technology, and incorporating some of the same components--crystal and copper, and so much more.

Finally, after months of trying different solutions, I had the hardware parts all worked out. I had consulted informally with a few people along the way, but basically (outside of programming) I had done it all myself.

Now, I could finally sit down and design a crystal handle with the rubber manufacturer before casting a die. It needed to be able to grip each crystal firmly after inserting the circuitry. I never knew there were so many different types of rubber content, polish and variability. Did I want shiny or flat looking rubber? Did I want high malleability? How thick or thin the rubber, and what color? The options were vast. I hoped I made the right choices. I had no partner to help make those decisions with me. I walked through the warehouse, wanting to examine all possible options. I questioned the manufacturer until I suspected he never wanted to see me again. No one had ever come to him with such a weird request—yet his patience was infinite. After a few weeks, I held a rubber holder prototype in my hand, and it was a thing of wonder and awe. It had two chambers and everything fit perfectly. The crystals made their final connection to the Whole.

I eventually decided to test what was coming through the hooked up crystals when we ran the Codes through them in a vibrational mode. Since what was coming through the crystals was pure information and non-Hertzian in nature, unlike definitive waveform frequencies, I had no idea what would show up on an oscilloscope. Would there be coherent patterns or something else? I called in an independent calibration expert to test all the programs and see for myself. He seemed somewhat stumped at first to learn we were not trying to run conventional frequency patterns. Then he became intrigued as he saw the crystals and I explained about the multi-tiered algorithms. What indeed did highly compressed information look like? He, too, wondered.

The waveforms on the oscilloscope showed all different signatures, no frequent or coherent patterns, which would be more consistent with individual frequencies. Instead, what it showed was a signal consistent with all the thousands of different types of algorithm codes, or random vibrations, that made up each program we ran. Amplitude, or signal strength, was low between 1.5 – 2 volts. We were trying to transform vibrational information into the frequency domain for measurement and found we could.

With the crystals attached, we knew it would pick up the transmission. Crystals can receive and send complex waveforms anywhere in the EMF (electromagnetic field). The first radio was a crystal set with a wire that touched a quartz crystal and picked up the signal. Crystals create a very fine and pure waveform known as a sine waveform. And sine waves have low voltage signatures, which was what our measurements had showed

Recently, I came across the Japanese designer, Tokujin Yoshioka, who grew a large slab of crystals over a six-month period for an art exhibit. Throughout the entire growing process he exposed the growing crystal to the music from Tchaikovsky's ballet *Swan Lake*. The tonal vibrations and pulsations materialized inside the crystal affecting its final form. In essence, the music information stored inside the crystal left unique markings, that grown crystal would usually not display. Just like Masaru Emoto demonstrated that intention could affect the crystalline structure in water, information also affects hard crystals.

Kathy J. Forti, Ph.D.

Chapter 12
THE POWER OF INTENTION

"Your life is what your thoughts make it." – MARCUS AURELIUS

For decades, scientists believed that our genes determine and control our biology. We have now entered the age of "epigenetics" which totally changes the accepted belief structure. Epigenetics means "control over genetics." We are learning that our genes are not our destiny. Our DNA is not set in stone, but our genes can be influenced through environmental factors such as stress, nutrition, and emotions—and even more amazing—these genetic modifications can be passed on to future generations. (Reik and Walter 2001; Surani 2001). Only about five percent of cancers and cardiovascular disease can be attributed to defective genes or heredity. (Kling 2003; Jones 2011; Seppa 2000; Baylin 1997).

So clearly, something greater is at work here in affecting how our cellular body responds to the information we are taking in either environmentally and/or emotionally. Bruce Lipton pointed out in his groundbreaking book *The Biology of Belief* that cells are programmable, like personal computers. Our beliefs control our biology, and the mind controls our beliefs. So can intention be more powerful in the long run than any possible form of conventional Western treatment?

Back in my little world, I was shown that the final components of this device I developed would magnify user intent based on one's biology of belief. I didn't understand this at first. Lipton was still working on his book when I was discovering this component and I had never heard of epigenetics.

What I discovered was that, like a search engine that calculates the type of data you wish to come up based on an imprint of prior search intent, energetic devices can pick up on this and start displaying signs of artificial intelligence. I was shown that in time the energy field of the user would become one with the energy field of this device. The key was not necessarily belief, but intent.

I experienced this first hand at a family gathering to celebrate my aunt's 86th birthday in Chicago. For the occasion, my sister flew back from Bali, where she lived most of the year. She arrived with some kind of Bali flu bug that incubated on the long transoceanic flight. She was wiped out and had absolutely no energy to do anything. She claimed her muscles and bones ached, but she didn't want to disappoint my aunt by being sick during the visit. I brought out the technology I had been working on and hooked her up. My sister had never tried out the technology, didn't know what to expect, and neither did I. I put together a 60-minute program that addressed all the symptoms she experienced and hoped for the best. I left her lying down on the couch, a crystal in each hand, hooked up to the signal box and ran the computer program. I left the room, so as not to disturb her, and went to talk with my aunt.

One hour later she came into the kitchen looking all bright-eyed. "How do you feel?" I asked.

"I feel great," she responded, "let's go do a museum." I looked at her, thinking she was kidding me. Museums take energy, and she looked like she was on her last leg just an hour earlier.

"Very funny," I said.

"No. I'm not kidding," she stressed. "I feel all energized and ready to go. How about the Art Institute?"

I had never seen anyone make such a turn-around that quickly and I was skeptical. How had it happened, or more important what had happened? I wondered if there was something she wasn't telling me.

"Did you do anything different when you did the session?" I asked.

She shrugged. "I just held the crystals and said, 'I am open to healing'."

A light bulb went off in my head. This was the intent amplification my Guides had been trying to tell me about. She had no expectations going in, but simply expressed an openness to receiving. Receiving is something a lot of us have trouble with. Giving is easy, but truly allowing the healing to take place requires a letting go. Acceptance also entails submission to a higher power. Being open to receiving opens a very powerful conduit. Unfortunately, on an unconscious level, some of us don't think we deserve such a gift. We consciously say we want to be healed, but can actually block it from happening by our underlying negative beliefs. What I learned was that you had to ask your own guidance to come in and work with you, and you had to really want to heal from a soul's perspective.

"This is a spiritual device," I was told. "It will allow the person the opportunity to connect with their own divineness, should they be open to it." I now completely understood what this

meant. While my Guides were in charge of the internal mechanism of this technology, they remained fairly open in allowing me
to incorporate my own design concepts of its look and feel. The
only thing they were emphatic about was that the technology
should NOT have any scanning, diagnostic, or testing ability. It
would just be a one-way delivery system. It would not be biofeedback in nature, where it scanned for health information and
gave back information in the form of numbers, percentages, or a
diagnosis. That might be okay for other devices, but not for this
one. "You humans judge yourself too much by numbers," I was
told. "This is not about judgment, but about connecting to your
own higher guidance and your own divineness."

I understood this on many levels. Too often, test results lead
to us to thinking ourselves into the very illness we are trying to
avoid. If test results tell us we are unwell, we can become unwell,
even if we were feeling great prior to the test. The mind is a very
powerful thing.

I had fun playing with intent and discovering our potential
unlimited nature. In late May of 2011, I was in London on
business with a colleague and proposed taking a side trip to
Stonehenge, then on to the Glastonbury/Avebury area to go crop
circle hunting. I was fascinated by the elaborate designs that
showed up in the fields of this southern area of England for
centuries. Some reports and drawings go back as early as 1686.
Aircraft just made them easier to spot in present day.

I knew some crop circles were man-made fakes, and I also
knew some were very real. An elaborate golden spiral called
"The Julia Set," because it resembled a mathematical Mandelbrot
fractal called by that name, appeared in a field opposite Stone-

henge in the light of day on July 7, 1996. One guard reported taking a fifteen minute break and coming back to see a crowd of people pointing at the adjoining field, and there it was, where it hadn't been 15 minutes earlier. One taxi driver and its occupants pulled alongside the field with a few other cars to witness a swirling cloud of mist with space between the ground and mist as it moved over the field. The 912-foot long formation took 20 minutes to create and was perfect in every detail. Such daytime sightings are indeed rare. No one knows for sure who is doing them or why, but speculation abounds. I, like many, was also curious and wanted to check it out.

My colleague and I decided to have some fun and see if we could try and influence the creation of a crop circle through conscious intent. (I love experimenting and playing with energy to see what's possible.) I didn't know if we would be successful or not, but I thought I had nothing to lose by trying. So, we decided to focus on creating a crop circle that would be personally significant in design. We didn't visualize any particular design. We simply put out the intent that it would speak to our own inner desires and we would personally recognize what it meant.

The prior February (in 2011), a few colleagues and myself had planned doing a two-week journey through Egypt to visit the sacred temples and pyramids. It was something I've always wanted to do, and the time seemed right to finally do it. Six months before we were to depart, I was warned by my friend, E.M. "Gene" Nicolay, that there was some uncertainty around me actually going on the trip. He saw a strong possibility of unrest in the area during that time, which might cause the trip to be delayed. He suggested I get full trip insurance just in case, which I did. Then, two weeks before we were getting ready to leave, Egypt erupted in chaos. With non-stop rioting in Tahrir Square, the Hosni Mubarak government eventually collapsed. Travel became too dangerous, and all trips to Egypt were cancelled. I was very disappointed, but glad I had taken the warning and gotten travel insurance.

When my colleague and I started thinking about creating "our" crop circle, we decided it would somehow make up for the great Egyptian adventure we never had. We focused our energies on the Avebury near Wiltshire area, where we were scheduled to visit. On May 28, 2011, right before leaving London, a crop circle appeared in a barley field called The Sanctuary right near the ancient monument of Silbury Hill in Avebury. It was one of the first of the season. Approximately 600 feet in length, it was comprised of nine circles of different sizes spread out in a long line that spanned the farmer's field. Crop circle analysts likened it to a planetary alignment configuration.

On the day we arrived in Avebury, May 30th, which was two days after the original formation appeared, a rare occurrence took place. Whoever or whatever created the crop circle returned to add more to its original design. Such rare events are called "Phase 2" occurrences, and it means pay attention to what has been added. What was added were two step pyramids much like the first pyramid built in Egypt—the step pyramid of Djoser, which we had planned on visiting. One was upright over another inverted pyramid with a circle cap atop each one, and they were placed, prominently, right in the middle of the crop circle formation. One pyramid for my colleague, and one for me. We were getting our Egyptian adventure, just as we desired, and the timing was perfect. We were elated. I had always been intrigued by the early step pyramids built in the Third Dynasty. The five-tiered step pyramid of Djoser at Saqqara was the first pyramid ever built and pre-dated the Great Pyramid at Giza. Our crop circle step pyramids seemed to pay homage to those astronomical beacons known as "stairways to heaven."

We followed proper crop circle etiquette and were careful to not trample the design in the barley field. Larger than our height span, we were each able to lie down in our own pyramid capstone with plenty of room to spare. I envisioned connecting with the real pyramids through the energy of the crop circle. It felt quite energizing, yet peaceful at the same time. The Wiltshire area of England where so many of the world's crop circles appear has prominent levels of chalk in its soil, which geologists believe attracts geomagnetic anomalies due to its electromagnetic qualities. It also attracts daily scrutiny from a nearby military base. Black helicopters flew low over this crop circle while we basked on the ground in its energy.

You could say this particular formation was man-made or man-influenced. We knew it was in answer to our thoughts and intent, crazy as they might sound to a lot of people. Intent can be very powerful, and when more than one person sets his/her mind to something, it takes on even greater proportion. To this day, no crop circle analyst has ever been able to explain the significance of those two added step pyramids.

Phase 1 - Crop Circle at The Sanctuary, Avebury, UK on
May 28, 2011

Phase 2 – Inverted Step Pyramids appeared two days later
on May 30, 2011

Phase 2 – Inverted Step Pyramid Close-Up

In the world of quantum physics, it has become clear that the observer *does* affect the outcome merely by being a part of the equation. The mind has unlimited potential whether we are praying for someone, rooting for a loved one to succeed, or trying to create physical crop circles in England. I recall how I tested this concept even before I knew it existed.

When I offered neurofeedback training in my clinical practice, I witnessed this up front quickly. During a neurofeedback session, clients hooked to EEG wires would sit in front of a video monitor, trying to move little Pac Man images on the screen by making faster, more desirable brainwave activity. No hands, just the power of their minds. I could see on my own EEG monitor what the client's brainwaves looked like, and when I got bored, I would play with their brainwaves. I wanted them to score higher, so I would silently think to myself: "Come on. Make more beta waves" and almost immediately, they would. A whole big burst of beta waves worth. If I kept up my internal cheerleading mantra for them, they were able to sustain the beta waves longer. Were they unconsciously picking up my silent cheering section on their behalf? Almost certainly. We are all constantly transmitting and receiving information from each other all the time.

However, some of us may be more adept at transmitting information than others, even though we all have the capability. I worked with a rather large population of military personnel and their families when I had my clinical practice in Virginia Beach, Virginia (home of the U.S. Atlantic Naval Fleet). Oftentimes, after working with military personnel receiving neurofeedback therapy, they might get transferred to a new location or base. If I could, I would find them someone in their new location and give them the customized neurofeedback training formulas that had successfully worked for them.

Twice, I had former clients call me and tell me that the clinician that I sent them to in the new city didn't make them feel like they had when they trained with me. These other neurofeedback clinicians had the exact same equipment I had and used my formulas, yet the effect was different. This is why most research studies are potentially flawed. They fail to take into account the negative or positive effect the observer and/or research team may have on the subject. This is even evident in placebo-based studies. An interviewer or technician, or even the nurse/assistant administering the pills in a drug trial, can all have an effect on the patient and the outcome.

Why are some very promising studies unable to be replicated by other researchers and, consequently, often dismissed as invalid? Because the human transmission factor is overlooked and conventional science has found no way to factor in this variable. Until it does, we will always get only half the picture.

Kathy J. Forti, Ph.D.

Chapter 13
HEART & SOULWARE

"Success is not final, failure is not fatal. It is the courage to continue that counts." – SIR WINSTON CHURCHILL

In July of 2009 I was ready to debut this new technology after almost five years of work. I was instructed to call it Trinfinity8, a merging of the words trinity + infinity coupled with the number eight symbolizing rebirth, regeneration, infinity, and for me (since I was born on the 8th), a symbol of success. I successfully finished my magnificent obsession, but was clueless whether any of it would actually work on anyone other than my family or me. For all I knew, it could turn out to be Kathy's great folly— something that terrified me. Throughout this whole process, I fervently prayed, "Please Dear God, do not send me on a fool's mission." I did not want to be associated with anything that didn't work or have meaning. I had certainly experienced a myriad of fake promises and products in my life, like everyone else. Integrity, honor, and truth were very important to me and still are. As a therapist, I taught ethics not only to my patients, but other therapists as well. This would be a life lesson and test for me.

I had to put it out there and find out if five years of work had been worth all the anguish. No paychecks, living off my inheritance, and almost penniless after all the costs of development had taken its toll. I had no idea software development could be so expensive. Yet, in the end, I found out I had more endurance than I ever imagined, or perhaps some might call it insanity. So like a mother birthing its baby, it was finally delivery time. I was led to debut it at International Society for the Study of Subtle Energy and Energy Medicine (ISSSEEM) at their yearly conference in the Denver, Colorado, area in July, 2009. All the well-known scientists, physicists, and researchers in the energy field were present at this forum. I had never exhibited anything before and didn't even know what exhibitors were required to do at such conferences, but I was determined to learn.

I secured myself a booth, set out two laptops running Trinfinity8, and offered free 15-minute sessions to anyone interested. I thought of it as field research. At that point, Trinfinity8 was in its first simplistic software incarnation (a debut release), and nowhere near the extent of what it offers today. I told no one that the technology had come out of a near-death experience. People thought it was an energetic device for anti-aging and had never seen anything like it—crystals and all.

Within a short period of time, I had a line at my booth that no other booth had. People were getting off a session and then dragging their friends over to watch and experience it as well. That's when I noticed a few of them pointing at the field around the people on the Trinfinity8 and whispering very excitedly amongst themselves. I can feel shifts in energy, but I am not one of those gifted individuals who can easily see such things. I came over to find out what they were witnessing.

"I'm seeing chards, like glass, coming out of the body," reported one woman. Another woman confirmed it as very sharp and jagged in nature. I looked over the shoulder of the person they were referring to and saw that the Release Emotional Blockages program was playing. I found that very interesting. It appears that negative and/or stuck emotions look like broken glass on extraction.

"Ooh, now I see this beautiful plumping coming out of the body," she said, referring to the same person after a few minutes. Again, I looked to see what program just kicked in and saw it was Balance Energy Centers, having to do with alignment of the body's seven chakras. I was fascinated and began scribbling notes. Something was clearly happening, and some people were feeling it as well. Some of the more adept energy practitioners started reporting some rather unusual experiences on the system that left me speechless.

An optometrist named Jon came off his session with tears in his eyes. I was concerned and asked him if he was all right. He then told me that he was also a medical intuitive, and while on the Trinfinity8, he saw all his own guidance come forward and fine tune the focus of his abilities, much like a radio dial finding the best reception. He said he had never felt such a profound sense of clarity before and thanked me for it. But he was not done yet. What came next totally astounded me, for this man knew nothing about the device or me.

"I saw a host of light beings, which is the intelligence behind this device," he said. "It was incredible. Then I saw a man step forward and identify himself as your father. He told me to tell you that he is very proud of you and that it was money well spent." I immediately burst into tears. That week was the anniversary of my father's death, and the words 'money well spent' was a typical saying of his. My father's words from beyond were clearly giving me support and confidence.

Another woman reported experiencing contact with a departed loved one during a session. I was beginning to wonder what kind of device I had brought forth. While my Guides had led me to believe it was a spiritual tool, all along I had thought it was really an anti-aging device. I would soon find out it was a clearly turning out to be both. One woman came back the next day to show me that her skin tag had dissolved after doing a skin clearing program. Silently, all I could think was, "Thank God THAT program works!"

People began asking me what they could or should experience while on Trinfinity8 or afterwards. I had to tell them I didn't know. It was different for everyone. Some might just experience an incredible feeling of peace and calm, while others had profound emotional, physical, or spiritual experiences. People soon began asking where this device had come from. I heard my own Guides prompt me, at that time, to reveal the truth of its origins. I knew I was not the inventor--they were. I was merely the developer, or messenger, who had brought it to form.

A member of the ISSSEEM Board finally came over to experience the Trinfinity8 after hearing all about it from several others. When she was done with her session, she smiled and said thank you. She had felt energy going to different parts of her body, followed by meaningful symbols that spoke to her personally. Then, she told me that in the early 1990's, Dr. Elmer Green, the father of Biofeedback, co-founded ISSSEEM because he saw into the future where such devices like Trinfinity8 would surface and help to change the landscape of energy medicine. ISSSEEM was created so there would be a welcome forum to introduce and support these emerging technologies. She told me that key organization members had been waiting and watching for a long time for such a device to finally surface. When they saw Trinfinity8, they immediately knew Elmer's prediction had arrived. This explained the large amount of visitors and re-visitors to my booth over the three days I exhibited.

Soon after Trinfinity8's debut in 2009, I was invited to exhibit the technology in Toronto at the Canadian Energy Psychology Conference. Dr. Sabina DeVita, a local female psychologist who was using Trinfinity8 with her clients, was also there exhibiting. She had combined the use of Trinfinity8 with a testing device called the Gas Discharge Visualization (GDV) camera, which had been approved by the National Institutes of Health (NIH) and the FDA in the U.S. Invented by the Russian scientist, Dr. Konstantin Korotkov, this electro-photon imaging device utilizes a weak electrical current applied to the fingertips, prompting the body to respond to this stimulus by emitting a glow discharge. This is then translated into graphs where you can see weaknesses in the energy field, which correlate with physical problems in the body.

Dr. DeVita used the GDV as a diagnostic instrument, then used Trinfinity8 to address the energy weaknesses in the body that were showing up. She had been very successful with this and showed me her progress. During the time I was there, a mother brought her teenage son over to the booth and asked that a GDV be done on her son. She "confidentially" divulged, without her son's knowledge, that something felt "energetically off" about him. She herself was an energy practitioner and wanted to see if anything would show up on testing.

After the GDV test was conducted on the teenager, Dr. De-Vita pulled me over to look at the test result images. She pointed to an odd, almost cord-like attachment to his energy body. "What's that?" I asked. I hadn't seen anything like it on her other clients' testing pictures.

"Some kind of energy attached itself to this boy and is weakening his field," she said.

I frowned. The skeptic in me emerged. "How do you know it's not some kind of spiritual or angelic presence?" I responded. She shook her head. "That has a different signature and it doesn't drain the body's field. This appears to be a negative entity."

"Okay," I said, not knowing how I could verify any of this. Dr. DeVita was a worldwide trainer for the GDV so she felt confident in her analysis. She then turned to me and asked, "What Trinfinity8 programs would you suggest for entity removal?"

I hadn't been ready for such a request and my expression must have shown how much I was taken off guard by it. She was perfectly serious. I had no idea what program to prescribe, so I went inside and asked my Guides. I was given a very clear message: Six minutes of Release Oppression (to get rid of negativity), followed immediately by six minutes of Divine Alignment (inviting one's own divine energy to come in and replace darkness). It was a 12-minute program. Would it do anything? I had no idea, but I was willing to give it a shot.

The teenager, who had never seen his testing images with the cord-like mass attached to his field, went ahead and did the 12-minute protocol. When he was finished, I asked him what the experience was like for him. He answered, "Pretty cool. I feel kind of lighter." It was an interesting choice of words.

Dr. DeVita immediately did a Post-GDV on the teen, and the attached "entity" was no longer visible. I filed it away in my mind as a possible fluke or testing error, until I had a conversation with a doctor in Northern California who told me he heard me mention this story and tried that same 12-minute Trinfinity8 protocol on another teen facing similar problems.

The teenage boy and his family had just moved into a new house, and from the start, the boy did not want to sleep in his own room at night. He wanted to sleep in the parents' room, even if it meant sleeping on the floor. Now, anyone with a teenager knows this is very abnormal behavior. Something was terribly wrong. The boy couldn't explain his need to sleep elsewhere, and his grades at school started dropping. He was depressed and anxious, and the parents sought out counseling for him. It didn't help.

They wondered if something in the house was affecting him. They did a little research, and learned someone had committed suicide in their son's room. Not surprisingly, the realtor had never mentioned it. They decided it might be helpful to bring in someone to help clear the negative energy possibly lingering in the teen's room, but even though it felt somewhat better afterward, the boy still did not want to sleep in there, and he continued to have trouble sleeping deeply anywhere in the house.

The boy's father mentioned the situation to a doctor friend who happened to own a Trinfinity8. The doctor offered the boy's father free sessions for his son to see if it would help. He decided to use the "entity removal" protocol my Guides gave me in Toronto. The doctor reported back to me that, by the second session, the parents reported that their son was "like his old self again." He was back to sleeping in his room, and even his teachers noticed a marked improvement. He was more focused at school and appeared happier. The father, who was also a baseball coach, told the doctor that he noticed something totally unexpected after the two "entity removal" sessions. His son's baseball coordination dramatically improved as well. There is no definitive explanation why his coordination improved, but I do know that sometimes when the spirit body is better aligned, the physical body can manifest changes in unexpected, yet positive ways.

When I think of these negative attachments or entities, I think back to some of the unusual patients I had over my early years doing psychotherapy and wonder if, had I the technology then that I have now, would things possibly be different for those people? Back then, I refused to acknowledge the existence of the dark forces of nature. I believed that if I surrounded myself in positive light that I would be safe. I didn't understand that there are always two polarities to everything: positive to negative, light to dark, matter to anti-matter, etc. They both need each other to exist for learning. This hit home when a new client came to see me one day, a young woman in her early 30's, who had small dark bugs that would come out of the corners of her eyes. I saw them and wanted nothing more than for her to get out of my offices as quickly as possible—taking her bug infestation with her. She scared me, because I didn't think such anomalies were possible. I didn't know what to do. This was beyond my scope and training. But she was clearly in distress and had been shunned by so many others. No doctor was able to help her or determine the cause. Not surprisingly, she was referred to psychotherapy.

I have no idea what led this poor soul to my particular offices, but I felt like I couldn't desert her, too. I asked her how and when this first happened. She told me she had been at a party, doing a host of recreational drugs, feeling euphoric, and floating when she heard a male voice near her ear ask, "Hi, honey. Can I join you?" She was feeling so good, she replied, "Sure" and felt something push into her. By the time she realized what she invited in, the entity clearly did not want to leave. She shamefully confided the bugs sometimes came out of other orifices of her body as well. She thought of killing herself if she couldn't get rid of it. She was forever fighting off the desire to do drugs and felt it stemmed from this one party incident. This is one reason I avoid any type of drugs. Heavy drug use, as well as alcohol, can leave people open to uninvited entities that feed off such substances—especially if the person has a weakened etheric energy field around them to begin with.

I worked with this woman for another two sessions before I could bring in someone who had a specialty with such cases (believe it or not there are such people), and her therapy resumed with the new therapist after a joint session. I don't know what happened to the woman, but it was my first real experience with dark forces. I always felt like I needed to energetically cleanse the room and myself after each of her sessions.

So it made me very happy to know that an entity removal program, using the Trinfinity8 technology, was not only available for such problems, but was used successfully. This same entity removal program has been effectively used on houses and businesses as well. One very intuitive Trinfinity8 practitioner in London, England, where the houses are so old with history it's not unusual to have a spirit or two lingering around, made a rather successful business of using Trinfinity8 to house clear negative entities. One entity even caused a crystal to fly up in the air, shatter, and break as it left.

Users often report feeling pulsing, tingling or heat sensations in their hands when the codes come through the crystals. If other crystals are also in the room, it can ramp up the energy even more, as crystals appear to communicate with other crystals and develop an in-sync mode. An interesting thing once happened while I was in the south of France in Nice doing several talks. I stayed with psychologist Dr. Marion Ross and holistic psychiatrist Dr. Tracy Latz who both use Trinfinity8s in their practices. Dr. Ross brought me down to her meditation room and showed me two large tower-like crystals that had once been strikingly clear and were now a clouded, milky white. A day earlier, she had run the Trinfinity8 near them and within a short time afterwards, the crystals had both visually changed in unison to a milky white. Her two auxiliary tower crystals absorbed the Trinfinity8 algorithmic Codes like a powerhouse storing information. It took several days for them to release the information and become clear again. It was an astounding thing to witness.

So, once again, when people ask me what they can expect from Trinfinity8, I often tell them to expect the unexpected.

Chapter 14
THE FOUNDERS

"We are made of star stuff." – CARL SAGAN

I am often asked about these beings of light that I connected to in the tunnel. Where do they come from and what is their true intent? Do they have names? Names are not important to them as, together, they function as one mind. It is my understanding that they come from the higher 8th dimension and beyond, which are unified dimensions of the highest light and spirit and form the basis of our concept of the Trinity. These are dimensions where pure thought and pure creation are infinite. Here, Christ energy is held in its entirety, and beings that exist on it work for service to others not self. It is the highest plane of perception and consciousness an entity can evolve to.

These beings call themselves "the Founders." They are part of the original souls that came into being and have been instrumental in the earliest beginnings of our race here on Earth. This seems to fit with the "panspermia" theory professed by Sir Francis Crick, that our DNA is far too complex to have originated on Earth and could only have originated from a higher intelligence from space, not from meteorite matter. Francis Crick and James Watson were co-discoverers of what has been called the greatest scientific breakthrough of the 20th Century-- discovering the double helix structure of our DNA. Interestingly,

Crick was under the influence of the hallucinogenic LSD when he had a cosmic vision of how our DNA helix worked. This altered-state vision led to his and Watson's unraveling the mystery of life. As a result of their discovery, they went on to win the Nobel Peace Prize for Physiology or Medicine in 1962. Up until his death in 2004, Crick still held firm to his panspermia belief that our DNA did not originate on Earth.

It is my understanding that the Founder beings were instrumental in "seeding" the original human race (and genetic variations thereof), as they did for many other races throughout the galaxies. The God creation stories are based on them. They placed humans within this dimension as guardians of Earth. These beings do not need to, but have the ability to, see and feel what happens in this and related dimensions on this planet. And they do, from time to time, bring the highest form of guidance by beaming this information (in light form) through to our grid. In rare instances, they can also act as Avatars, and will incarnate in lower dimensions, such as ours, in order to bring new evolutionary patterns into being. Since these beings have fully developed their 12 strands and even 24 strands of DNA, they are distinct, but also are a unified energy field. In essence, they are already at the stage of being one with God or All That Is, meaning Source. They are Higher Consciousness.

Our origins did indeed come from our star brethren who made adjustments along the way, confounding the scientists looking for the missing link between apes and modern man. Ancients referred to these star brethren as "the Gods" and were often depicted in ancient art as having wings (meaning they came from the skies), even though many religions have interpreted these beings as "angels."

The Founders and other Higher Consciousness beings come to be of service only during keys points in our evolutionary cycle, which is right now. Earlier points in evolution dealt with man's physical, emotional, and intellectual changes and advancements. Neanderthal's brain was not as advanced as Cro-Magnon's, and modern man (homo-sapiens) has developed even further. Many of these earlier versions co-existed alongside each other, as evidenced in conjoining burial sites. It appears some form of ethnic cleansing occurred leading to Neanderthal man's demise and a more evolved version of Man came about, as we know it.

The Founders' principal concern now is the evolution of the dimensions, particularly this dimension, and not only the planetary bodies, but also the souls found within it. The inability of this realm and the souls in it to ascend in the evolutionary process has far-reaching implications throughout the multi-dimensional universe.

E. M. Nicolay, in *The System Lords and the Twelve Dimensions*, claims that the repeated inability for a planetary system to ascend can eventually cause it to become a "fallen" system where it collapses in upon itself. In other words, when souls cannot ascend in the universal evolutionary plan, it eventually terminates itself, dying from lack of energy over many millennia. He goes on to say that this evolutionary process within dimensional sub-levels happens every 26,000 years, but every 250,000 years there is the opportunity for the entire Universal Dimension to ascend.

While we are clearly at another major pivotal point in our evolution right now, this time it is for our spiritual soul. Our evolution affects the evolution of other dimensional realms as well. What we fail to grasp is that we are all inter-connected to every living thing. What you do to the least of your brethren, you ultimately do to yourself. Those who are out for their own benefit are missing the bigger picture. This is why the world is so polarized right now and extremism is seen in every form— especially played out in the religious and political arenas. Yet these very extremists most likely have no idea they are being extremists. They're not bad people; they just see what they are doing as right to protect their ideals.

We will always need both the dark and light sides for our life learning lessons to truly take hold, otherwise life would be without challenge. Where there are limited obstacles or challeng-es, there is little opportunity for growth. The more polarized the dark and light forces are, the greater the lesson. As souls, we are all playing our parts. Even Hitler played his part that ultimately brought forces together for humanity to change.

The Founders and other Higher Consciousness beings can't directly interfere with our evolutionary process due to our free will. However, they can lend some help to those who are open and are ready to receive it. They have a vested interest in what happens on Planet Earth. Earth contains some of the key dimensional portals that star brethren have used for ages to travel the galaxies. The Middle East region has one of the biggest portals--Iraq in particular and the Gulf of Aden. It's no coinci-dence that the most fighting has occurred there, even putting aside the much sought-after vast oil reserves that mark the area.

Evolutionary ascension is achieved through physical DNA development, since higher vibrational frequency that leads to ascension is held within the DNA. This acts as a key to opening the doors of ascension for the entire realm. As more strands of DNA develop and become visible, all beings within the realm are able to hold more light and resonate at a higher frequency. This higher frequency, or awakening consciousness, is in essence the key to opening the doorway into the next evolutionary dimension.

The origin of souls is different and not all are working on behalf of the human connection. The Founders aren't the only ones here. There are factions that don't have our best interest at heart and continue to sow the seeds of discord to keep man, in essence, enslaved and incapable of evolutionary ascension. These other beings feed on fear, power, and control. There is a war being waged on many levels right now for our very souls. Fear is a tool used to control the masses. Fear stops a person from growing consciously and attaining higher realms. It prevents one from growing in Divine Light. And ultimately, it prevents human ascension.

As more people awaken in their awareness and begin seeing through the lies and deceit around them, it becomes harder and harder to control the people and make them drink the fear-laced Kool-Aid. In the 4th dimension, whatever you think and feel happens immediately, so one needs to face one's fears in this 3rd dimension and release them now before one can, in essence, graduate.

Did I know all this before my near-death experience? Certainly not. It was a slow awakening for me as well. My near-death experience was never meant to be my final exit. It was an opportunity to connect to something greater than myself and make a change for not only me, but hopefully to help others as well. Although I had heard about "the tunnel" countless times, I didn't know or understand then that the tunnel I found myself travelling through on the way to the Light back in 2003 functions as an energy conversion device. Earth vibrates at a slower, denser frequency than other dimensions. In order for the Founders to work with me, it required my old guidance exiting, and my energy body being sped up with a higher vibration inside the tunnel to receive and work with these new Guides.

This project was part of my pre-birth contract. Whether one believes or not in the concept of reincarnation, it is my understanding that I had done similar work just prior to the 3rd and final upheaval and demise of the continent known as Atlantis around 10,500 B.C. Trinfinity8 is based on Atlantean technology using today's current technology, which we call personal computers. During these Atlantean times, I worked within what was the known as the Temple Beautiful (which would be later brought to Egypt by the Atlantean priests). In the Temple Beautiful, crystals were used to resonate and affect the physical body. This knowledge came as no surprise, since I had been having dream symbology of such events for years. In this lifetime, it was part of my soul's purpose to return and to assist people by re-creating those methods used in ancient times, but using today's emerging technology.

The second year I went back to attend and exhibit at the ISSSEEM Conference, an older man I didn't know came up to me after receiving a Trinfinity8 session. He said he remembered this technology from Atlantis and didn't think he would see it again for several more lifetimes. He reported experiencing a deep sense of connection and the overpowering feeling of coming home.

I learned that Atlantis was even more technologically advanced than we are today. They had their own version of modern-day computers, but faster, simpler, and inter-dimensional in nature. The common link was that they also used crystals (which they called "firestones") to transmit, store, and receive information. Archeologists have come across some of these ancient data storage devices, but have no idea what they are or how to decipher and open them. They are light-based, consciousness, computer-like devices that have to connect with corresponding like devices to activate. To many, they will look like pretty translucent ornaments—and yes, they have crystal properties. They are programmed with binary code, because the ancients are the ones that gave us this language.

It quickly became very evident to me that we are slowly rediscovering and re-learning what we already once knew. Centuries ago in Atlantis, they understood that each person has their own unique resonance or healthy vibrational signature, which identified them in the universe much like a fingerprint does today. Every signature is different from everyone else's. There is no such thing as a standard set of frequencies that would cure and/or fix all. This is why many frequency-based devices today are only partially effective. They don't know and cannot accurately read the person's unique frequency signature.

The Atlanteans knew not only how to read each person's vibrational signature, but they could detect when the energy body became unbalanced, leading to disease states in the physical body. With this knowledge, they could transmit that person's unique healthy signature back to them to re-boot and re-align their system. This would be much like using a "restore point" on today's computers. Crystals were predominantly used in this re-alignment process in order to resonate the body back into a state of attunement.

We won't see this technology re-emerge for identifying human vibrational signatures any time soon—at least not in our current 3rd dimensional reality. It is clearly 4th dimensional in nature and requires a higher consciousness state of the race using it. This is because in this 3rd dimensional realm, it could be used as weaponry against a person. True compassion is needed to work with this "restore point" technology. It takes more highly evolved souls who are not set on war, power, and destruction. This is why no being of light from another dimension will be allowed to bring it through to this realm. And do not believe anyone who says they already have the capability to read someone's unique resonance and restore them. There are many false prophets out there.

The Founders have given us some of the universal healing codes found in the mathematical algorithms of the Trinfinity8 technology as a safe starting point. Other similar technologies will quickly follow. I am not the only one who was seeded with this information. Even the universe hedges its bets in case a primary choice candidate doesn't, for one reason or another, make it to the finish line in a timely enough manner.

I remember hearing from someone about a man who had similar mathematical algorithm information come through, but he got stuck on the delivery process. He may have totally dismissed the concept of crystal transmission and eventually abandoned the project. So far no other energy-related device has used this particular delivery method. This time, I'm proud to acknowledge that a woman made it to the finish line first. This may be why the divine feminine is being seen more and more as the bearer of universal change.

As I have already stated, similar technology to Trinfinity8 was also used during Egyptian times after the fall of Atlantis. Crystals were used to generate power for their technologies. The reason Atlantis fell was because certain Atlanteans were tuning the resonance of the crystals too high in order to accelerate power capability. This caused a build-up of frequencies, which led to a destructive break-up of the forces in the earth, which ultimately caused a ripple effect throughout our planet. Today, this would be likened to setting off several nuclear bombs along California's San Andreas Fault line. The destruction would be mammoth.

Many of these same Atlantean souls reincarnated and were prevalent during the reign of Amenhotep IV, known as the Pharaoh Akhenaten, in the 18th Dynasty of Egypt. This was a key evolutionary point in time for man, much like right now. The shafts of the Great Pyramid were aligned with the key star systems of Sirius A and Sirius B, which make a full revolutionary cycle around the Earth approximately every 25,950 years before it comes back into re-alignment. When alignment was precise, the Great Pyramid at Giza was used as an ascension portal for those beings moving from 4th dimensional density to 5th dimensional, in order to move closer to Source. A space-and-time portal opens during this alignment. Some might know it better by the term "Stargate."

Due to Atlantean knowledge, science was much more sophisticated during that time. But, this knowledge was held in the hands of only a few select groups. The Great Pyramid was connected to the Earth grid and also served as a way to generate electromagnetic energy. The top of the pyramid, which is now truncated, once had a capstone made of solid gold. Gold is the most efficient and non-corrosive conductor of electricity. While the Great Pyramid was used for many rituals and ascension-based initiation rites, the primary purpose of it was for re-alignment of earth energy grids and to generate power.

The Ancient Egyptians used the pyramid to act as a resonant cavity to send sound waves directed throughout the Earth that would echo back creating an electrical wave. The steeply slanted mysterious Grand Gallery of the Great Pyramid, which is a passage less than 7 feet wide, 153 feet long, and 29 feet high, provides a key. They would convert these Earth vibrations into electricity using resonators in the Grand Gallery to produce certain tones. One can wonder if it was similar to today's Helmholtz resonators (discovered in the 1800s) where acoustic reverberation results in self-sustained oscillations. These pyramid resonators might have been used to reduce or screen out unwanted tones, becoming a tuning station only for Earth grid frequency tones resonating at F#.

In 1899, inventor and visionary Nikola Tesla discovered this same electrical phenomenon that would allow for free transmission of electrical energy around the world. He called it "terrestrial stationary waves" and discovered it directly corresponded with three acoustic frequencies that had an exact Fibonacci ratio. It meant that the entire planet could be used as a resonant tuning fork, making wireless transmission of electrical energy and telecommunications possible. Even back then, he saw the world as one day being completely wireless and the Earth grid providing the electrical energy to power it. Mathematical law and acoustic frequency were the answer. The Atlanteans had already discovered it centuries ago and brought it with them to Ancient Egypt. Tesla was merely re-discovering a long-known secret of nature.

Unfortunately for history and mankind, Tesla's benefactor at the time was the banker J.P. Morgan. When Morgan heard about the possibility of free energy, he immediately shut down all funding to Tesla, letting him know that if he couldn't put a meter on it and make a profit from it, Morgan wasn't interested. He buried it and made sure the idea would remain buried for quite some time. Over the years, many have tried to bring forth this technology. They were stopped through a clandestine campaign of intimidation, professional ridicule, dire threats to themselves and their family, and financial ruin. Think about it. Such technology would no longer leave us dependent on gas, coal, and oil for energy. Ultimately it would change not only the face of the world, but of all mankind.

Free energy for everyone has always been possible. The Egyptians knew it and used the King's Chamber and the rest of the Great Pyramid as a resonant tuning chamber. Egypt's Temple of Dendera glyphs have always fascinated modern-day electrical engineers. The wall art with "djed" pillars look suspiciously like a large light bulb held by high-tension voltage insulators. Two "technician" like figures, wearing eye goggles and some kind of earphones, stand alongside this giant light bulb. A few floor lamps with cable wires can also be seen in other glyphs.

The suggestion of the use of electricity in ancient times has also been found at other locations. Several objects with traces of electroplated precious metals seem to point to the use of an ancient type of electric battery.

The sides of the Great Pyramid were once smooth limestone casing that were stripped away long ago. This great edifice looks nothing like it did back then and much of what it was intended for has purposely been shrouded in mystery.

During Akhenaten's time, these select groups who held most of the knowledge of the stars, and who some were believed to have descended from star beings, used the Great Pyramid to re-boot and re-align the Earth's energy grid points. The Great Pyramid sits in the exact center point of planet Earth. It was no coincidence the ancients picked that exact spot to construct the Great Pyramid. They could only have known that this was the earth's center point from those who had already charted the far reaches of our planet from the skies—our star brethren—who came in different shapes and sizes.

Traditional science doesn't seem overeager to question why some of ancient skulls found in 1928 by Peruvian archaeologist, Julio Tello--now known as the Paracas skulls--are so unusually large and elongated. Ancient drawings and texts show that these beings were very tall, almost giants by today's standards. Akhenaten was said to be 14-1/2 feet tall and his sister, Nefertiti, who he took to wife to protect the royal bloodline, was reported to be almost 10 feet tall. You can see it in their drawings as well. Historians have explained it away as a "cultural perspective," as if the artists of that time couldn't draw accurately what they were seeing. But no other pharaoh or king was depicted this way. You will see some of these large, elongated skulls displayed in South American countries as well, especially in the museum in Lima, Peru, but never in the United States. It brings up too many questions about our ancestry that many would prefer not be addressed.

While it is well known that some cases of skull elongations are the result of intentional cranial deformation from head binding, not all fit into this category. In early 2014, it was reported that DNA analysis was finally conducted on one of the Paracas skulls which showed no intentional cranial deformation. Final analysis showed it had mtDNA (mitochondrial DNA) with "mutations unknown in any human, primate, or animal known so far." The geneticist conducting the DNA analysis concluded that they were dealing with a "new human-like creature, very distant from Homo sapiens, Neanderthals, and Denisovans."

Who were these people with such modern day technology? Are they the missing link in our evolution? The most well-known drawings of elongated skulls appear during the reign of the Pharaoh Akhenaten. Akhenaten was a master Avatar. He descended from star brethren. He attempted to change the priests of that time from the worship of many gods to monotheism (one God or the Law of One) and was met with extreme resistance. He looked to the "Sun" as the God of Life, which would later be misinterpreted by religions throughout the centuries to mean "Son of God." Akhenaten is the most misunderstood figure in Egyptian history and was vilified for his attempts at enlightenment—mostly by the priests of the time who feared losing their powerful hold on the people.

Akhenaten was deeply involved in dimensional ascension technology using the Great Pyramid for initiation rituals and rites. He was totally committed to this process and was the enlightened Jesus figure of his time. Unfortunately, things did not go well back then and man's evolution took a step backward. Many were deceived by a select few. Unfortunately, this process of soul ascension had somehow gotten corrupted by dark energy. Rather than helping souls ascend to avoid repeated earth plane incarnations, they were trapping souls in a dimensional limbo. A powerful few knew that what they were doing wasn't working, but didn't seem to care, as it fed their ego and self-aggrandizement. They convinced Akhenaten and his key followers (myself included) that what they were doing would be successful. By the time it was realized that something had gone terribly wrong, it was too late for those trapped souls.

We have been paying the price for that failure ever since. As a result, we took a step backward in our evolutionary process to 3rd dimension density and lost much of the scientific wonders and knowledge from that time. It also affected our DNA and created a mutation in our pineal gland. The pineal gland is our mind's "third eye." It is our personal link to the Stargate in our brain. Our total understanding of our divine heritage is stored in this gland, which is part of our endocrine system. Energy once flowed through this gland when our consciousness was more developed and expanded. It has, since our "fall" to 3rd dimension density, shriveled to the size of a pea, waiting to once again be opened and activated to a higher knowledge--and, to once again reclaim what is inherently ours.

Yet, all is not entirely lost. The Great Pyramid itself has stored much of this knowledge of our past. Unfortunately, it still resides in 4th dimensional reality, not easily accessible to us. That was approximately 26,000 years ago. Every 26,000 years, the Earth shifts into that same planetary alignment where certain dimensional portals once again open and evolutionary rise is possible. That time has come again. The ancients knew this from their star brethren. This is why they were so fixated on astronomy and the stars, and wanted generations that followed to be prepared.

The Mayans' own calendar, given them by their star brethren, also tried to tell us that another 26,000-year epoch would end on December 12, 2012. It wasn't the end of the world through destruction, as many believed. It was simply the beginning of the period that held an opportunity for great evolutionary change. Of course, modern-day prophets misinterpreted this time with doomsday Armageddon messages, missing the greater picture. We are being given another chance to get it right this time. The portals are open, and change is coming faster. If nothing else, it is an exciting time to be alive due to the expanding possibilities. On a soul level, we have all contracted to be here during this time to witness this consciousness change.

Because Akhenaten failed during the last epoch and was deposed because of it, the Great Pyramid was abandoned for ascension purposes. While it took almost 100 years to build (10,490 – 10,390 BC), it was used for less than 50 years as a tool for mankind's evolution. It was sealed up, its purpose no longer necessary—a piano out of tune. In a sense, it has become a burial chamber for those trapped souls lost in a dimensional limbo.

During current times, we have the opportunity once again to put things right and put man's destiny back on track. We continue to be tested by souls who have not yet learned their lessons regarding the evils of war, greed, and aggression. I was told I would meet some of those very figures from Akhenaten's time and was to be vigilant of their intent and purposes. Some are already well known in the quantum sciences. They, too, have the opportunity to right the wrongs they perpetrated approximately 26,000 years ago; but a few of them, I have learned, are back to their old tricks, attempting to deceive the people with slightly skewed information. I have found inflated ego to be a predominant trait and a telltale sign. Yet, I have faith that they will rise above this in the end. After all, we are all in this together.

I was told how important it was to protect the integrity of the Codes. What can be used for good can also be used for ill purposes. Therefore, it came as no surprise when a few different individuals separately approached me wanting to piggyback their own inventions off the algorithmic Codes I was given. And often, they would want to change them just enough to fit their own power needs. Each time I said NO, despite the promises of money. Others told me I should give the Codes to everyone for free since they are gifts from God. To do this would also open them to manipulation and corruption. A certain responsibility is involved. Instead, monies go into service-oriented projects to provide for and help others. In addition, I helped develop a very inexpensive iPhone and Android app so everyone could have access to four algorithmic programs that could be beneficial to most people on a daily basis.

The Founders gave me a special prayer blessing that is said over every Trinfinity8 system that is sent out. Prayer is a conscious interface with intent. This is very important in setting the right foundational intent for its work in the world through its new owner. This blessing is done religiously by either me or my assistant and has been in effect since the very first system.

It was also the Founders' intent to have this technology reflect the feminine energy matrix, more so than the masculine. The Hindu religion believes that we are currently in the Age of Kali. Kali was the female destroyer responsible for stamping out the ignorance of man and ushering in change. Masculine energy needs to be balanced with the divine feminine energy to attain harmony. Some who have used Trinfinity8 technology, without knowing of my involvement, have commented that the energy felt "softer" or that "it must have been designed by a woman, because it's so simple to use." Trinfinity8 had no need for all the complicated maze of levels and layers, or the bells and whistles, which usually accompany other man-made devices. Its simplicity speaks for itself. I remembered the old adage, "Less is more." And as time went by, I found that there was more to this technology that even I hadn't suspected. Could it push the envelope in ways that made time and space irrelevant?

Kathy J. Forti, Ph.D.

Chapter 15
SEPARATENESS IS AN ILLUSION

"We are here to awaken from the illusion of our separateness."
— *THICH NHAT HANH*

I had already experienced firsthand from my Rife experimentation that we, as human beings, are all transmitters and receivers of information. We think of someone and suddenly we receive a call from him or her or run into them and tell them, "I was just thinking of you," or "I was just getting ready to call you. You must be psychic." Skeptics may call this coincidence, but quantum physics provides some more accurate answers.

In Michael Talbot's book *Holographic Universe*, he writes about a remarkable event that took place in 1982. A research team at the University of Paris, led by physicist Alain Aspect, performed what turned out to be one of the most important experiments of the 20th Century. "Aspect and his team discovered that under certain circumstances subatomic particles such as electrons are able to instantaneously communicate with each other regardless of the distance separating them. It doesn't matter whether they are 10 feet or 10 billion miles apart."

In 1997, physicist Dr. Nicolas Gisin of the University of Geneva duplicated these findings and found that subatomic particles appear to be communicating at the mind-boggling speed of 20,000 times the speed of light. He concluded that, regardless of the distance separating them, the reason they were still able to remain in contact with one another had nothing to do with being able to send some mysterious signal back and forth. The real reason was that their separateness was an illusion. At some deeper level of reality, such particles are not individual entities, but are actually extensions of the same fundamental something: the ONENESS factor.

In essence, all things in the universe are infinitely interconnected. Mystics from many different traditions, religions, and cultures have been telling us for centuries that we are all connected. No one is separate – be they a subatomic particle or a human being made up of subatomic particles.

I needed to do my own experimentation to understand the parameters of this technology I helped bring forth. Could it transfer information across time and space without any known mechanism as well? If so, everything had the capability of being wireless like Nikola Tesla had predicted. We might not understand how our phones and electronic communication devices receive info without wires, but we know it has the capability of doing so. Perhaps we need to think on a more global scale about human beings as wireless transmitters as well. I decided to put it to the test and the opportunity to do so quickly manifested.

My favorite Aunt Jo, who is in her late 80's and feisty as ever, lives in Chicago. I often phone her to see how she is doing. Several days earlier, she had been released from the hospital after undergoing a hernia operation. On the day I spoke with her, she had discovered her surgical stitches were becoming red and swollen--which didn't sound good. It was a Saturday afternoon, and she had made an appointment to see her doctor first thing Monday morning. She reported she wasn't in any real pain, but there was some slight discomfort. A post-operative infection was suspected.

In the course of our conversation, I asked her if she wanted me to send her some healing energy. Now, I knew my aunt had no idea what I meant by such an offer. She is clueless about the world of subtle energy and probably didn't believe in such things anyway. A strict Catholic, I was sure she thought I was proposing to pray for her. She said, "Sure"—more a throw-away response than anything else. But I had secured her permission, and that was important to me. She didn't have to understand what I was going to do, she just had to give me the go-ahead.

So the next day, a Sunday afternoon, I put together a program protocol that incorporated algorithms to help detoxify an infectious reaction as well as speed up recovery. I typed her name into the computer and was instructed by my Guides to write her name three times on a piece of paper. They informed me that multiples of three are very powerful in the energetic world. Ancient Greek Pythagoreans called it the "Sacred Geometry of 3's." I recalled how my Rife experiment, using two of my clients' names, along with my own on a piece of paper (three names together), manifested something I totally had not expected. Was this part of that theory?

I was told that the Ancient Greeks received this knowledge from the Egyptians who reported receiving the secret alchemy of 3's from their star brethren "gods." The Ancients believed "3" symbolized transformation. The alchemy of 3's is seen in the Trinity (Father, Son, & Holy Spirit). Within the alchemy world, they knew that if you added two different elements together, it created a third entirely different element (1+1 = 3, i.e., black, white, grey), which was entirely different from the first two original elements. This is the science of alchemy, and it can create unknown, but sometimes magical, outcomes.

If one decides not to use the "Sacred Geometry of 3's" with the person's name when doing long distance healing, another way to also enter the energetic field is through pictures. A photograph contains the complete subtle energy info about the individual. The more recent the photo, the better the imprint of their energy in the here and now, and the greater the potential for the individual depicted to receive the energy information I was sending. I knew this on a subconscious level. I flashed back to trips I had taken in primitive countries. The natives would turn away and not allow you to take their picture. You were a stranger to them, and they believed a photo could capture their very soul essence. I had always thought it was a superstitious belief on their part, but now I began to wonder if their belief held some deeper element of truth. After all, there is a lot about our world that we simply don't know or understand.

Using both a photograph of my aunt and her name (x3), I put together a 60-minute protocol for her, which I hoped would be helpful. An hour-long protocol is somewhat excessive, but my rationalization, at the time, was that since there was a vast distance between Chicago and Los Angeles, it needed to be longer to be stronger. I now laugh at that misconceived notion. Aspect, Gisin, and even Einstein had already discovered that, in the quantum world, distance is immaterial. I clicked on the Run button to start the remote healing program and went off to do my own thing.

At no time did I ever volunteer the method or specifics of my experiment with my aunt. Nor did she know the date or time I carried it out. I did not want to get her expectations up or look foolish in her eyes if absolutely nothing happened. I was clearly safe to keep any possible failure to myself. I knew it was best to remain neutral about the outcome. I had nothing to lose, and she had everything to gain if something good really happened.

I called her Monday evening, assuming she had already seen her doctor. "What did your doctor say?" I asked

"Oh, I cancelled the doctor," she said matter-of-factly.

"You did *what?*" I asked, not knowing if I heard her correctly.

She laughed. "Well it was the darndest thing. I came home from playing bingo with the girls (no illness would prevent her from her Catholic women's club meetings), and I decided to take a quick shower. Just as I was getting out of the tub, I suddenly felt these flu-like symptoms hit me from out of nowhere, and I thought to myself—oh, for crying out loud, now I'm getting sick, too!"

"What time was that?" I asked.

"Somewhere, around four o'clock." There was a two-hour time difference between our cities, and I had run her program around 1:00 p.m. my time (3:00 p.m. her time, and it was a 60-minute program). I had to know more.

"What did you do?" I prompted.

She explained that when these symptoms hit her, she felt extremely tired and wiped out--a clear detox reaction, I thought. She then went on to describe how she decided to lie down and take a quick nap, only to be shocked when she slept through the entire night and did not wake up until the next morning. My aunt is a night owl. She almost never gets to sleep until after midnight. I remembered to take note that a 60-minute program might be too much energy for an 80-plus-year-old woman. And I might have to scale down protocol time length as well.

"When I woke up this morning," she continued, "I noticed all the redness and swelling around my stitches was totally gone. It was amazing. And, I had all this energy so--I cleaned my house." She seemed quite impressed with herself. "Since the infection seems to be gone, I cancelled the doctor. I'll see him in two weeks instead for my regular visit."

This was my first unofficial one-subject long-distance blind study. She had no knowledge of the method of transfer, the time, nor scope, and was not trying to get better to please me. Of course, I finally told her what I had done, and even though she still doesn't understand how it all works, to her credit, she approaches it with an open mind. Now, whenever she has some ailment and I ask her if she wants me to send her some healing energy, she always answers, "Oh, honey. You can send me anything you want."

In 2013 I had the chance to help her again. I had just finished doing a five-day Bali Spirit Festival in Ubud, Bali, where I was asked to speak. In conjunction with the talks, we offered free 20-minute Trinfinity8 sessions to everyone that came by our Healing Hut at the festival, something I always insist on doing. Most of our visitors were other energetic practitioners and healers who would come back each day for repeat sessions and report feedback on what they noticed. After the festival, I was tired from working long days outside in the humid heat of Bali and was ready for a welcome break.

Three of my friends from the Los Angeles area--Judy, Agnes, and well-known medium James Van Praagh (my fellow Machu Picchu, Peru, travelers)--had asked me to meet them in Sydney, Australia, for a cruise where James was teaching a workshop. I agreed, since I was already in that part of the world. On my way to Sydney, while making a connection in the Singapore Airport, I learned that my Aunt Jo had been rushed to the hospital having suffered a heart attack. I fretted when I wasn't able to reach her, since I was in transit and would be getting to the cruise ship in Sydney just in time for sailing.

I had not mentioned the situation about my aunt's condition to James, but since he speaks with dead people all the time, he often hears news from the other side first. He was the one who told me, "Your father is here, and he says they are all watching the situation very closely with his sister." I knew he was talking about my Aunt Jo. "He says she can't make up her mind whether she wants to stay or go. If she decides to go, tell her they will be there to help her cross over."

I have some pretty interesting and unique friends, and conversations can be very off the wall at times. At the next port, I was able to reach the hospital and get my aunt on the phone. Her voice was very weak; she said she was not doing well and couldn't talk long. I related what James said my father (her brother) had said about her needing to make a life or death decision. She was fascinated that James found out about her through my deceased father. Amazingly, her voice got stronger, and she perked right up at this news from beyond. I then asked her if she wanted me to send her some healing energy. "Yes," she said without hesitation, thanking me.

I immediately put her on a specific protocol to help align her with her soul's purpose and Restore Vital Force, if it was right for her. I knew it was not my judgment call to make about whether she stayed or passed on. I felt I was helping send her energy, so she could make that decision clearly. I played the protocol I made for her continuously for two days via long-distance session. Two days later, to the amazement of her son and her doctors, she was released from the hospital and went home. "We almost lost her," my cousin told me. "I was sure she wouldn't make it through this time. She could barely move."

When I got her on the phone at home she sounded like her old self again. "You tell your father I'm not ready to go yet!" she informed me with a laugh. It was her desire and intent to at least make it to her 88th birthday. I'm happy to say she has successfully passed that milestone as of this writing.

PLANETARY & GROUP HEALING

I was invited to address an energy practitioner's group in San Antonio, Texas, during June of 2011. When I arrived, I noticed how deathly hot it was and how all the lawns and foliage were burnt from lack of water. I learned that Texas was in the midst of one of the longest drought spells it had experienced in years. Even the golf courses were yellow and brown from lack of rain and sprinkler water. Water was severely rationed, and rain hadn't been seen for over a year. Both people and nature were suffering.

Whenever time permits, I like to do a group Trinfinity8 session for the people and the area. Everyone gathers in a circle, holding hands with a crystal rod at each end of the circle linked to a Trinfinity8, playing a session protocol for whatever the group's intention might be. At times this can be quite powerful, as you feel an energetic current pass from one person to another in a continuous loop. The group becomes a charged conduit, which has brought forth some profound experiences from participants over time. A group mode can be anywhere from two people to 250, as was tried with a nurses' group in San Diego, California.

The San Antonio group wanted to focus on bringing rain to their area and asked me if I had some sort of rainmaker program in Trinfinity8. Unfortunately, I didn't have such a program. This is when I saw a picture in my head of San Antonio as a systemic body whose lymph system was blocked and/or backed up. It needed to get bodily fluids moving. I did, however, have a program called Rejuvenate Lymph System which seemed to fit the problem at hand for helping move fluids in the body. It was certainly worth a try. I used that program and a few others to help relieve the heat, and we focused on bringing relief to their parched city. Two of the people in the group had their own Trinfinity8s. One was from Austin, Texas, and the other from San Antonio. They decided to immediately follow-up remotely, running both San Antonio and Austin using a satellite picture of the Texas area and the protocol we had put together. A few days later, I got an excited phone text saying, "Look at the Weather Channel for Texas." When I checked it out, I saw it was raining steadily ONLY in the San Antonio and Austin areas. Their drought spell had been broken after almost a year. I couldn't help but laugh with sheer pleasure.

The first time we used Trinfinity8 to work with Mother Nature was in April of 2010. My office manager, Tracy Andersen, brilliantly suggested the idea of sending help to the Gulf of Mexico after a massive oil spill. Thousands of gallons of oil were hemorrhaging into the Gulf waters each day and the situation was dire. The very concept of using the technology to help our planet Earth literally gave us goose bumps and chills. My Guides sent the clear message: "Now you're getting it!" It was a big moment for all of us when we finally understood the "bigger picture."

We asked Trinfinity8 owners all over the world to use a map of the Gulf of Mexico and put together a protocol which would assist a severely compromised immune system. Our planet's ecosystem was in serious jeopardy. Two days after we started running the waters of the Gulf around the clock, they finally capped the well. The skeptic in me always acknowledges that it could have been the prayers of everyone in the world that helped stop the destructive flow. After all, we are all in this together to save Mother Earth.

So we tried it again in March of 2011 when the nuclear power plant at Fukushima, Japan, began spilling toxic radiation into the air, soil, and ocean waters. Like before, it also took two days after we started as a group for them to finally cap the biggest leak. Coincidence? Quite possibly, but then a strange thing happened. Our office started getting calls in the middle of the night. No message, just a static sound. They were all calls from the same number. I didn't recognize the country code, so I looked it up and discovered it was the country code for Japan. And the city code for the number placed it in the Fukushima Prefecture area, not far from the nuclear spill facility. I was curious to see who and why they were calling our California offices in the middle of the night and not leaving any message. There was an obvious time difference, so I waited until later in the evening to call the number to find out. A Japanese person, speaking some English, answered the call. They said they had no idea who I was or why their phone had been calling our phone. Sometimes you just have to shrug your shoulders and accept that the universe works in strange and mysterious ways. There was no logical explanation. A weird cross-circuitry in telephone lines, perhaps? I like to think it was Japan's way of saying, "Thank you very much. Energy transmission received." The area still has so much more healing work to be done. Sometimes, it feels like we work on a triage basis--addressing areas that need extra help immediately. Earth is in need of a lot of continued help, and the Founders always seem quite pleased when I and/or other Trinfinity8 practitioners focus on problem areas affecting our beloved planet. After all, like us, it is also a living organism that deeply appreciates our love and care.

In 2013, I could see the situation in Syria was really heating up. U.S. President Barack Obama surprised the American people by threatening a pre-emptive missile strike on Syria. Many could not understand his reluctance to wait the few extra days for the final UN Inspector's report verifying which fighting faction was really behind the Syrian chemical weapons attack. It was a recipe for disaster.

I was shown many of the true forces at work behind the scenes causing havoc, which could only lead to another devastating World War 3. Violence only begets more violence. War is almost never the answer and it was hard to trust our government after the lies the Bush administration perpetrated on Iraq. It was time to start running Syria on Trinfinity8 to help send peace and hopefully bring about a compromise regarding the crisis situation. Again, two days after we started running Syria, the UK Parliament said "No" to supporting U.S. military involvement in the area. As we continued running peace programs throughout the day, Obama then decided to wait and attempt to get Congressional approval for a missile strike versus politically going it alone. We continued running programs, and soon Russia was proposing an agreement with Syria to eliminate their chemical weapons as a way to stave off further escalation in the area. We know we were not the only ones praying and sending light energy to the situation to help turn it around. The amazing thing was that it took almost destroying our world for partisanship to be tossed aside and for Republicans to agree with Democrats or Democrats agree with Libertarians or Tea Partiers, on the same issue that affects the entire human race. NO MORE WAR. Enough. We as a people have had enough. We can change our world by working together rather than working against each other.

Through experimentation, we have started to learn the extent of the power of these algorithmic Codes given to us, whether they are used for physical, emotional, and/or spiritual attunement. The Founders created programs that we soon discovered could be used literally as well as figuratively. The Reduce Inflammation & Swelling program can be used not only to help decrease inflammatory tissue problems, but also inflammatory "issue" problems, such as those dealing with anger and violence.

Diminish Brown Spots (something that sounds purely cosmetic in nature) has been used to help clean out infestation problems, and for one owner had an unusual result: "I started running Diminish Brown Spots on our house," she reported, "and my husband suddenly started cleaning out all his old dirty junk from the barn. I was totally floored." She had been after him to do this for years without any success.

A holistic psychiatrist, used the Lips program for her client, and it helped her client to become more assertive and speak up for her own needs. Energetically, it addressed the entire mouth area where energy was blocked.

We learned the Stimulate Appetite Suppression program was not for just dieting, but addressed all appetites. This was accidentally discovered after a cigarette smoker, wanting to lose weight, used this program and afterwards said it made his cigarettes taste nasty—something he hadn't expected. As a result, we started using it successfully with other substance and emotional addictions.

One of the spiritual programs, called Heart Resonance, was designed to open the heart to giving and receiving love and forgiveness. Accidentally, we discovered it was also beneficial for physical heart issues as well.

When I went to Peru in June, 2012, to take place in the Winter Solstice ceremonies on Machu Picchu with Peruvian Shaman Mallku and my friend, clairvoyant medium James Van Praagh, many in our group of 45 were feeling the effects of the 12,000 ft. altitude. Lack of oxygen and sleep, shortness of breath, racing heart, and freezing temperatures at night, which lodge in your chest and cause coughs and colds, all add up to a weakened immune system. After two weeks, we were all starting to feel the effects of what I termed "Stairmaster Zen-Cardio" hiking. James suggested a group Trinfinity8 healing session. It was only intended to be a 15-minute protocol to help clear lungs and sinuses, but it turned into something totally unexpected.

Many in the group were either highly intuitive, psychics, or mediums that worked directly with deceased individuals from the other side--like James. A few reported that, soon after the group joined hands and the Codes started transmission through the rather large circle, they felt a surge of energy as their own guidance and deceased love ones moved forward, curious at the energy coming through to the group. It was reported that many deceased Chinese healers came forward and started working on each group member, using James as a channel. The energy in the room was incredible, and James began working at a very fast pace on each member of the group. A few reported sinuses or coughs clearing immediately, while others reported feeling 100% better the next day after finally being able to get a night of restorative sleep.

Over time, I found it not that unusual that Trinfinity8 will sometimes attract higher energy beings or healers from the other side to check it out when it is being used. There is a sense of cosmic connection. My Guides told me early on that many people's inner guidance would know immediately what this technology is for, even before the individual consciously recognizes it. If they're not ready for it, they will pass it by. It is not for everyone.

People simply like how it feels—even pets are no exception. Animals respond to subtle energy, regardless of the fact they have no idea what it is or how it works. Pets are a good example of "beyond the placebo effect." Pet owners often report pets displaying out-of-the-ordinary behavior when their owner or someone else is on Trinfinity8. Cats that are not lap-sitters suddenly want to come over and sit next to the computer or plop themselves on the user's lap and start purring. Dogs will come over and nudge their owner until they put the crystals on their pet. A dog will often stand perfectly still for as long as 5-10 minutes until they have had enough and then walk away. It was a natural progression that people would eventually start using Trinfinity8 for pet ailments such as injured ligaments, skin rashes, digestive problems, trauma, etc.

I will never forget one pet owner telling us how her Westie terrier, Quincy Bubbles, had gotten into her private stash of decadent dark chocolate raisin brownies and eaten all four of them. Most animal owners know that chocolate is toxic poison to dogs (even cats) and can make them very sick, leading to possible death. Dogs can't metabolize the theobromine stimulant found in chocolate, like humans can. It affects the nervous system and the heart muscle and often causes cardiac arrest. Knowing this, they immediately rushed Quincy Bubbles to the vet to have his stomach pumped. However, the brownies were so dense, they got stuck in his stomach and pumping wouldn't work. Quincy Bubbles was admitted to ICU for intravenous fluids and observation. The veterinarian told them it would only be a matter of time before his kidneys shut down and his heart would develop fatal rhythms. The vet did not expect the dog to survive the next 24 hours. The dog's owner started running an intensive Trinfinity8 program on her dog overnight. After 24 hours, the vet was astonished to find that Quincy Bubble's blood-work showed no signs or symptoms of heart or kidney failure.

The words "amazing," "no explanation," and "baffling" were used to describe his recovery. The Trinfinity8 sessions continued every two hours throughout the hospital stay. Quincy Bubbles was released in excellent health after another 24 hours and, the next day, even the vet was amazed that he had come through it.

Animals respond and so do children. These are both interesting groups, because they also come into the "beyond placebo affect" category. Neither has a conscious investment in the process, whether it is for themselves or to please their parent or owner. I have watched countless attention deficit hyperactivity children immediately fall asleep when they get on the Trinfinity8 and Balance Energy Centers is used. It helps bring them to a more balanced level of energy where it feels so foreign to them that they immediately fall asleep. Three minutes later, when that particular program might be done running, they often wake up. They always appear to be re-set and calmer. Parents are amazed they can even sit through a session. We have some practitioners that are working with severely autistic children and noticing improvement in these children's lives as well. It does not take away their autism but it does help improve social stability, greater eye contact, the ability to allow being touched, and brighter mood. For some parents and children, this means the world to them.

Trinfinity8 is not a medical device. It does not "cure" disease. However, it helps shift the body into a higher vibrational state where all healing and rejuvenation is possible. Then, the body can do what it's naturally intended to do, which is function optimally and prevent disruption of energy in the subtle bodies from manifesting in the physical body. Encouraging as that may sound, it does not short circuit or prevent a person's karma. It is my experience that sometimes people need their illness as part of their soul's growth plan. Trinfinity8 is not a magic bullet for everyone.

It has always been my belief that to work on an individual requires their permission, whether it is in person or with long distance energy transmission. We come into this life with life lessons we have already laid out to learn. Someone else didn't plan these lessons for us, we agreed on the game plan coming in. We have flexibility within that general game plan, allowing for free will and choice. We would learn nothing if everything was set in stone beforehand. Neither would we learn and evolve if we consciously knew what options we were supposed to pick that would guarantee a positive outcome. It's obvious that some of us take on harder tasks than others in order to accelerate our soul growth. We can't take away another's lesson plan by always trying to help or cure them—especially without their conscious approval. Some people really need their illnesses to learn.

This was evident when one elderly woman with Parkinson's disease discovered her tremors stopped after one Trinfinity8 session. She experienced tremors for most of her adult life and unconsciously defined who she was by her affliction. She expressed to her therapist that she didn't know what she would do without her tremors. She thought they would be with her until she died, and I'm sure her life was laid out accordingly in her mind, based on this premise. With this belief, it came as no surprise that her tremors returned after several days. She was not yet ready to let go of them, and on some level, be it conscious or unconscious, she believed life would no longer feel safe and familiar to her without them. The thought was too scary and so healing was blocked off.

Trance medium E.M. "Gene" Nicolay once shared with a group of Trinfinity8 practitioners how he was asked to help a therapist working with a woman who was having a difficult time healing. She had an inoperable brain tumor that was not responding to any traditional or alternative treatment, even though she fervently prayed and professed wanting to get better. When he psychically tuned in to her energy body, he came across a troll-like energy guarding this particular area in her brain where the tumor resided. The "troll" energy told him the woman had put this blockage there for the specific purpose of eliciting empathy and understanding from her family, who had disempowered her in various ways throughout her life. Until this family issue was addressed, no help to the tumor would be allowed through. Without healing the emotional/spiritual body first, the physical body will always remain in an unbalanced, healing-resistant state. Unfortunately, most traditional Western medicine only looks at healing the physical body without ever addressing the root spiritual cause.

Sometimes it is hard to understand why some people have to endure horrendous challenges in life, be they physical handicaps, traumas, abuse, and/or illnesses. When I worked at the New York City Ronald McDonald House, a home away from home for those being treated for cancer at Memorial Sloan Kettering Hospital, I met a young African-American girl from Georgia named Jenab meaning *angelic spirit*. Jenab was about 10 years old when she was diagnosed with osteogenic sarcoma (bone cancer) in her leg, which necessitated amputation. She often discarded her prosthetic leg and would hop around the Ronald McDonald House on her one good leg, laughing, making mischief, and seeking out avenues of fun like most children do. She spent hours one afternoon corn-rowing my hair with colorful beads so I would look like the actress Bo Derek in the movie *10*. It tickled her enormously to get her hands on my long thick hair and work her magic. She had a real talent for braiding, making friends and you just couldn't help but love her. Everyone did.

When we received word at the Ronald McDonald House that she died, I invited all the children there who knew her to share their fondest memories of her. We laughed and we cried remembering her antics and felt her spirit very close by throughout our storytelling. That night I had a very vivid dream about Jenab. In the dream, I saw her approach me dressed in a long white and purple African print ethnic dress with a matching turban-like head wrap. I had never seen her wear such tribal attire, and she looked absolutely regal. She was quite excited and happy to see me, and her smile was contagious. Without hesitation, she lifted her long skirt to proudly show me she had both of her legs back again, and could run, skip, and even dance. To prove it, she did a little soft shoe for me.

"Please tell my mother I am doing well, having fun, and have met up with many old friends again," she instructed me. "Tell her not to be so sad." I promised her I would pass on this message, and then she shared with me an amazing thing—the purpose of this lifetime on Earth. It was to be a dual lesson for both her and her mother. Jenab shared that she spent many lifetimes being so independent and self-sufficient that she believed she never needed the help of others. She had not fully learned to accept the selfless love and giving of another—or to be reliant on another human being for daily acts of nurturing and kindness. In this lifetime, her mother became her teacher. Jenab contracted, on a soul level, to have a debilitating illness, bone cancer and an amputation, to truly experience and know this need. Looking back over her life, she felt like she accomplished her purpose and mission.

For her mother, she told me it was a different learning experience. Instead of learning to receive like Jenab, she was experiencing the value of what was important. It became an exercise in deeply loving and selflessly giving to another, yet knowing your time together is very limited. Where many parents might become so devastated after a loss of a child that they emotionally retreat into depression and despair, part of her mother's soul lesson was to accept that cherished gift and be able to continue giving the same nurturance to Jenab's younger surviving sister. These life lessons for growth can be tricky. Hearing Jenab explain it made me realize that early childhood deaths are never some karmic punishment for the parent(s), but often an opportunity for accelerated soul growth due to the emotional sacrifice involved. Jenab's mother was a very intelligent, career-oriented executive in the political realm. Divorced and raising two children on her own, her whole life took on a new direction with Jenab's illness, and afterwards as well. It also made her stronger.

I delivered the message to Jenab's mother, who was very open and receptive to a message from beyond, and was quite grateful I had passed it on. "She was like this little old soul in the body of a 10-year-old," she recalled of her daughter. "Sometimes, I wondered who was the adult and who was the child."

When I described the attire Jenab wore in the dream, she told me that Jenab's father, a native of South Africa, had brought back that very same ceremonial outfit for her a year earlier. It had been Jenab's favorite, and she only wore it on special occasions.

I often think of Jenab when I hear of someone with a chronic or possibly terminal illness. I realize I can only help them so far. Everything is a process. I can't take away their karma; I can't short-circuit the lesson they came here to learn; I can't cure them. The only thing I can do is give them support to quite possibly work through the learning process faster by helping loosen the energetic blockages that prevent true healing from occurring. The rest of the work, they have to be open and willing to do themselves.

The same holds true whether you are a psychotherapist doing counseling work or an energy practitioner doing healing work. You have to help the client get out of the way of themselves so they can do their own work. There were times when I was doing therapy I had to tell people I couldn't help them and to come back when they were truly ready to change and/or do the work. The fastest route to therapist burnout is if you find yourself more emotionally invested in the client getting better than the client himself. They have got to want it more than you do.

There are what I call the "Buyers" in therapy--those who own their problems and take responsibility for their thoughts and actions. They are invested in the process of getting better and will do the work required. Then there are the "Visitors." Visitors are those just testing the waters. They think everyone else is the cause of their problems, and they are just there because someone either told them to go or made them get help. They generally want you to fix the problem and make it quickly go away. The key is to figure out early on who is a *Buyer* and who is a *Visitor*. A *Visitor* can be turned into a *Buyer*, but it might be a rocky road to get them there.

I am convinced that one of the greatest ingredients to healing is our belief. When I hear people say, "I can't" or "nothing works for me," I see that, in a way, they are celebrating a belief in a negative uniqueness. I tell them if they believe they can't, then they won't. No one can help them until they open themselves to healing. The mind is, after all, the greatest builder.

Chapter 16
TESTING THE POSSIBILITIES

"All life is an experiment. The more experiments you make the better."
– RALPH WALDO EMERSON

Life is ultimately a series of continuous tests. It was no different with this new technology. We were curious to see if the Trinfinity8 affected performance testing. We had individuals report back to us what they experienced running Trinfinity8 remotely on themselves while taking an important test, or a State Bar exam, a military physical and/or while even running a marathon race. Each reported doing exceptionally better than they thought they would. The military person tested was a Commander in the US Navy Reserves. This 55-year old woman reported doing a 15-minute Trinfinity8 program the morning of her test to help increase energy, muscle strength, and oxygen levels. She later reported back it was her best physical readiness score in over 20 years. As a result, her performance was graded Outstanding. Consequently, she did not want to tell any of her fellow officers what she used in order to keep her competitive edge.

The logical next question was: Does Trinfinity8 affect blood testing in athletes? We took that question to an Olympic coach who put together many different Trinfinity8 sports enhancement programs and used them on his athletes. He found that, yes, it improved their performance, but it could change blood testing.

Anything that changes blood raises an immediate red flag with anti-doping authorities, even if the results don't show positive for specific drug use. While this might be bad news for athletes searching out an untraceable non-drug competitive edge, it also shows that Trinfinity8 can cause a physical change in some people's blood. This was quite amazing news.

We wanted to know if it could also effect change in DNA. So we searched out a reputable scientist, Dr. Glenn Rein at the Quantum Biology Research Lab in Colorado to see if he could provide us with some answers. Dr. Rein experiments with DNA from human liquid placenta DNA. He developed new methods for testing subtle energy effects after scientists realized the old Newtonian physics methods of testing were insufficient for use in this new quantum realm.

We asked Dr. Rein to independently test three Trinfinity8 programs (Telomere Repair, Reverse Aging, and Divine Alignment) under resonance conditions using certain excitation frequencies to measure electrical conductivity. One method for measuring electrical conductivity of bio-molecules like DNA is to apply current at different frequencies and measure the response of the voltage spikes from 25-100 kHz. Two electrodes were placed in the DNA for this purpose.

Dr. Rein suspended the crystals rods an inch above the liquid DNA. The algorithmic Codes were then played through the crystals for 30 minutes, and the DNA response was measured using 15 different measurements. The same was done with a non-treatment control group, which did not receive the Codes. The results showed that the treatment group significantly increased the electrical conductivity of human DNA compared to the non-treatment control group, which did not. What did this prove? Increased electrical conductivity is associated with increased ability of DNA to repair itself (Retel, 1993), and repaired DNA has 20-fold higher conductivity than the same DNA when damaged (Hartzell, 2003). The results suggested that it was extremely likely the Trininity8 programs would have a profound effect on DNA and healing the body.

Of the three treatments, Reverse Aging caused a 50-60% stimulation in electrical conductivity, with Telomere Repair coming in second place. Divine Alignment, which has nothing to do with DNA repair, was tested out of curiosity and showed it would be least effective in affecting DNA, which was not surprising. We finally had some answers. Yes, Trinfinity8 could affect human DNA in a positive reparative sense. (The full results of this study can be found on the research page at www.Trinfinity8.com.)

Our next question was whether the benefits from the Codes lasted. Part of the answer to this came from an unexpected source. I gave a talk at the Bio-Energetic Conference in Greensboro, North Carolina, in October 2011. Our Australian distributor, Rasunah Alston, had an exhibitor booth at the conference and was giving free Trinfinity8 sessions to all attendees. She had three systems set up and a waiting line as well—something not that unusual when you exhibit something new and aren't charging a fee for the service like other vendors often do.

One of the exhibitors at the conference, a Dr. Michael Kessler of the group *Health Detectives*, was conducting his own unofficial testing project on different technologies at the conference using a new testing device (also out of Russia) called the Omega

Heart Rate Variability Test. The test uses the pulse at the wrist to test for five variables: (1) Cardiovascular System Adaptability; (2) Autonomic Nervous System Regulation; (3) Central Nervous System Regulation; (4) Psycho-Emotional States; and (5) Overall Health Index.

I happened to be at his booth, and when he learned I was affiliated with the Trinfinity8 technology, he asked me point blank, "What do you have in that device?" When I asked him what he meant, he showed me testing data he had conducted, unbeknownst to us, on those who had received sessions at our booth. In fact, he admitted intentionally sending people over for Trinfinity8 sessions so that he could test them afterwards for reliability. "Your device tests higher than anything else here, and I want to know why. What's in it?"

"Really?" I said, curious to learn what he had discovered. "Show me."

He pulled out one of many charts. The first was a 68-year-old man who, when they ran a baseline on him, showed a biological age of 76—eight years older than his chronological age. His Overall Health Index was at a very low 4% out of a possible 100%. This was before his 15- minute Trinfinity8 session. After his first session, his Health Index went up to 36% on his test results. Kessler had him come back the next morning to see if the testing results held, and they continued to improve overnight up to 42%, which confirms that energy continues to shift and gel over a 24-hour period after a Trinfinity8 session. So after his morning test, the man decided to go back and get his second Trinfinity8 15-minute session. He immediately went to Kessler's booth afterward for testing. This time his score went up slightly to 48%. At that point the man was curious what would happen if he had a session on a different type of energy device, which will remain nameless here. Upon doing this, his testing afterwards showed a drop down to 44% overall health. He wasn't happy with his slip in testing results so he went back to the Trinfinity8 booth the next day and asked that he get a session on the INTENSE setting level instead of the NORMAL level like he had initially. With his 3rd Trinfinity8 session on Intense, his test results showed an Overall Health Index jump from 44% to 67% and his biological age now showed him at 58, 10 years younger than his chronological age of 68. In two days, the man had gone from a very low health index of 4% to 67% and showed cardio-vascular, autonomic, central nervous system, and psycho-emotional balance at levels Kessler had never seen before in such a short time. The man also reported feeling better. "And there are more just like this," Kessler said, taking out the charts of other people he had tested on Trinfinity8.

We often tell people to wait 24 hours for any possible changes. Sometimes change can happen immediately with some conditions, while others may take a few hours for someone to notice a difference, or a few days later. Energy shifts can be gradual or immediate, and then the physical body has to catch up to adjust and make those changes noticeable.

A naturopathic doctor told us the story of his first introduction to Trinfinity8. He was visiting his friend in Beverly Hills, a surgeon who had added the Trinfinty8 to his alternative medicine practice. When he learned his friend had a new energy device that his clients liked, he told his surgeon friend, "Okay. Give me something I can feel." His friend put him on 15 minutes of the program Energy Boost.

He reported that, while it was a very relaxing and calming experience, it certainly gave him no noticeable energy boost as was intended. He immediately discounted the experience. Upon leaving, the office manager asked him what he thought and he shrugged. She asked him what the doctor had programmed for him. Energy Boost for 15 minutes.

She looked at the clock. It was after 6:00 p.m. She looked back at her boss wide-eyed. "Don't you remember? That has a two-hour delayed effect and shouldn't be given later in the day. It might affect sleep."

The surgeon and the naturopath both shrugged. The latter added, "Don't worry. I never have trouble sleeping." When the naturopath related the story to me later, he shook his head laughing. "Well almost two hours later, just like she said, it kicked in with a jolt. I was wide-awake and couldn't sleep. I was up all night reading about this device on the Internet. I now have great empathy for my clients who have had insomnia over the years. I always told them to have some warm milk, take a hot bath, relax, or read something boring. I never knew insomnia could feel like this. It was quite a humbling lesson." As a result, he figured if it could have such a profound effect on him, he wanted to know what else it was capable of doing and acquired his own system to further experiment.

The Codes did not come with a built-in manual detailing how it all works. The Founders pretty much left that up to us to discover for ourselves its true potential. With each new experimentation comes new insights and understanding. I have been told by some of the leading intuitives of the world that we haven't even begun to scratch the surface of what it can do. The beauty of it is that it is not standardized. It affects each individual differently on a very personal level, depending on where they are in their spiritual and emotional process. It finds what most needs work and goes to work there first, regardless of what you think you might need.

I heard many stories of people saying their eyesight improved without doing any specific eye program. They gradually noticed it when they realized they no longer picked up their glasses to read the fine print. I myself rarely use glasses anymore to read – only when the light is very poor and the print is very small is it even necessary.

An older woman named Janie called me one day, very concerned. Her beautiful silver grey hair, which she loved, was turning darker at the roots. At first, she thought it was her imagination, but her hair stylist confirmed it and wanted to know what she was doing.

"I'm not doing ANY Trinfinity8 hair rejuvenation programs," Janie insisted, "So I don't know why my hair is changing color."

I didn't know either. "What programs *are* you running?" I asked.

"I'm running Balance Endocrine System for adrenal gland support," she reported.

Oh—it now made strange sense. One of the key signs of adrenal exhaustion, due to stress, is premature graying of your hair. As her adrenal glands got stronger, her hair started growing back in its original color. This was incredibly astonishing. Then, others started reporting that they saw their hair color change or darken on the hair shaft first, not always at the roots. Change was not always the same mode for everyone. I didn't know what to make of it. Many of these women weren't even trying to make their hair color change, yet their bodies were attempting to turn back the clock. What is the signal mechanism for such a thing to happen? It seems like an impossible thing to change, yet we were shown pictures showing us otherwise. I personally never experienced that particular hair phenomenon, but then again, I rarely run those particular hair or adrenal support programs on myself. Now, perhaps if the Founders could give us mathematical codes to change our hair color to any shade we desired, I might be interested once and for all to stop dyeing my own hair.

Trinfinity8 attempted to turn back the clock in other areas as well. Older women were reporting an increase in their sexual libido, which they admitted "had been dead for a long time." One woman in her 70's lamented that she didn't know what to do with her new sexual drive, but she *had* noticed she attracted some slightly younger men at the supermarket these days. It appears when our sexual libido returns, so does the energy we radiate, which others can definitely pick up.

Chapter 17
PSYCHIC-SEXUAL TRIGGERS

"It's time we saw sex as the truly sacred art that it is. A deep meditation, a holy communion and a dance with the force of creation."
— *MARCUS ALLEN*

Sexual energy contains the creative life force. It is sacred energy. We can channel that energy either way—perhaps in a project that fulfills us or with a partner for sexual fulfillment. I myself noticed that many of the most profound experiences in my life had a sexual component. My parking lot rape by a stranger at age 18; my Monroe Institute astral sex experience in my 30's; my Rife frequency photo transmission experiments in 2004, where I took on a client's sexual addiction I didn't even know he had; even my dolphin encounter experience in the 1980's.

While traumatic or negative events, such as physical and sexual abuse, have been known to trigger latent powers the person might not have been aware they had (i.e., heightened perception, intuition), near-death experiences are more likely to bring about a spiritual awakening, or an all knowing. If the person has had one or more of these events at an early age, then the odds increase that with each traumatic event that occurs afterwards, psychic powers or psi ability will grow.

When I was six years old, I was bitten in the face by a neighbor's German Shepherd dog that just had puppies. Someone was supposed to be watching the mother dog while we visited with the babies, but she got distracted in the back yard, and the dog somehow opened the house's back porch door and came barreling down the basement stairs to protect its young ones. I instinctively put up my hand to ward the dog off, but she took it as a threatening sign and lunged at me, biting into my cheek and chin. Blood was everywhere. As they rushed me to the hospital, I saw my very short life flash in front of my eyes.

At that time, I had never heard about life reviews, and there wasn't a lot there being six years old, but seeing all the blood and my parents' terror, I thought for sure I was dying. This, I'm sure, prompted some region in my temporal lobe to kick into "end of life" mode. This internal program doesn't seem to always know the difference between really dying and thinking one is dying (perhaps due to possible futures?), but it still kicks in. The second time I had a life review experience was when I was raped and thought I might be stabbed and killed by my attacker. There appeared to be a pattern. Not the exact same review, but the mode and method were the same.

Years later, after technology had taken off, these life reviews reminded me of how certain computers are programmed to automatically either save stored data or start spewing out warning messages right before the system crashes. Are we as humans also programmed to start potential pre-death messaging? My rape near-death life review felt like a series of emotional snapshots happening at the speed of light. It also felt like a memory release. I'm not sure I've heard any of the near-death researchers theorize about the true significance of this particular "memory dumping" aspect of a life review. It is fascinating if, indeed, this is a key component of our soul's preparation to move into another dimension. One has to ask oneself if these events alter neural pathways forever, should we survive.

But what if there is a genetic factor, and these events are the triggers to opening our genetic heritage? What if family members also have heightened perceptual ability? My mother was somewhat intuitive and became a dowser later in life. She was only about 10 feet off from identifying where the water source was located when they looked for where to drill for the well on their country home. But going back even further, my mother once showed me writings of an experience my grandfather had as a little boy in the early 1900's. At the age of 10, he became extremely sick with some kind of high fever. The doctors told his mother they didn't expect him to live. In his writings, he talked about being propelled out into the universe, seeing a brilliant light, and being privy to a powerful God Source. He saw the planets, the stars, and what can only be described as some type of nuclear fusion reaction in space that was "blinding." When he returned to his physical body, the fever broke, but he was now blind in both eyes. The doctors told his mother there was no reason for him to be blind. His eyes looked perfectly fine. They accused him of malingering. His parents became impatient with him; his siblings ridiculed him. It took one month for his sight to finally be restored. During the time he was physically blind, he saw inwardly in his mind's eye many marvels that would later prompt him to devour science books and try his hand at inventing. My mother recalled him having a fascination with the spiritual world. I would not know any of this until after he had died, when she showed me his writings. I would have had a million questions for him. From what he wrote, it sounded like he had a very powerful near-death experience but had no context with which to explain it—as have many others like him.

Trigger events that unlock heightened perceptual ability usually come about in three ways: the individual hits puberty, they experience a severe trauma, or they find a mentor to train them. Since boys usually hit puberty between 9-14 years of age, and my grandfather was ten at the time of his experience, he had two out of three factors going for him. And once psi powers are opened, there is no sealing them back up. Your life will never be the same again. For years, I am told, he searched for the meaning to his experience. I have no way of knowing if he ever found it.

It's an interesting phenomenon, but near-death experiencers seem to be unconsciously drawn to other NDErs. But of course, you say to yourself. They've both been to the other side and now have some sort of built in OW-GPS (other worldly global positioning system) hard-wired in. Consequently, these people oftentimes are magnets for the strange and unexplainable. I wondered if this explained why some of the most unusual mental health case histories came my way as a therapist.

I had to ask my Guides, "why?" Especially in light of the psycho-sexual component to most of my own personal psi openings. The answer I received is that sexual energy can provide an opening or gateway to the higher realms of consciousness under certain circumstances creating "spiritual energy." Just to make myself clear, this is not an endorsement for having multiple mindless sexual encounters with strangers on a frequent basis. Sexual energy of that nature comes from the lower chakras and generally stays there, oftentimes getting trapped and creating physical problems in the body. My Guides were showing me that during Ancient Egyptian times, sexual energy was channeled to the higher chakras through the pineal gland. This energy had a direct correlation with resurrection, immortality, and heightened states of consciousness. The Egyptians called it "tantra" or "ankhing"-- the Sanskrit word for "essence" and/or "the strands of a braid" referring to the very matrix of life—our DNA.

Several years before I had my near-death experience, I had dreams of holding large ankh-shaped objects in my hand. In the dream, I would see my attention continually drawn to a gold ankh ring on my left pinky finger that had two additional symbols emblazoned over it. At the time, I had no idea what these symbols signified. They seemed familiar, like I should know what they meant, but I consciously didn't. I assumed they might be Egyptian in nature, and when I awoke from the dream, I looked up the ankh and found it was the "symbol of life." On a deeper level, I knew this was a superficial explanation. Ankhs are emblazoned on Ancient Egyptian temples everywhere. The priests held them; the pharaohs held them, and versions of these ankhs would later be seen in Coptic and Christian crosses for centuries long before the man Jesus walked the earth.

I kept coming back to the ankh images I saw in my visions. The ones emblazoned on the gold ring I wore within the dream. I drew all three symbols as I saw them in my mind, then did an exhaustive search to find some answers. I finally found the three symbols emblazoned together-- *the Ankh, the Was Scepter and the Djed Pillar*. What I eventually learned will not be found in any books. These symbols became camouflaged in mythology and falsely interpreted with modern religious significance.

Egyptian Was Staff, Djed Pillar, Ankh

The Sacred 3 (as I will call these symbols) were passed down to the Egyptians after the fall of Atlantis. I asked my friend E.M. "Gene" Nicolay to go into trance to obtain any deeper information on the significance of these multi-dimensional symbols. He reported back the following:

"They represent all levels of the human body--the physical body, the emotional (parasympathetic) body, the energetic (etheric) body, and the Soul. They also evoke the known elements of earth, air, water, and fire.

"The Ankh is the embodiment of the 'Tree of Life' representing resurrection and the continuing cycle of rebirth. The loop shape shows circular movement of the Soul, up around and beyond the line that represents physical incarnation and return of the Soul into the Staff of Life. It represents the flow of life and the blood flow within the physical body, which is self-perpetuating. What is imbued from above is then pushed below the horizon into the lifetime. It is a symbol for reincarnation and life-giving sustenance.

"The Was Staff is often interpreted as a symbol of power for rulers and Gods, but it is more accurately likened to the 'Staff of Life'. As a magician uses his wand to make magic, the Was Staff represents the Soul using the physical body to 'make magic' occur. The magic is life itself in physical form. It is the wand of creativity, self-manifestation, and pure alchemy.

"The Djed Pillar symbolizes wholeness and stability. The Ancient Atlantean architecture, particularly in its Temples of Beautification, where illness could be corrected through interac-

213

tion with a person's Soul, one would see four pillars facing the Temple's frontage. Each pillar represented an aspect of human beingness: The Soul, the Physical Body, The Energetic Body, and the Mind (Emotional) Body. Atlanteans used these four pillar structures to identify their most sacred temples. These temples represented the height of civilization and wisdom of that age, and the symbol for it was the Djed Pillar. On a more physical level it represented the spinal column as the temple of kundalini energy. They tapped into this kundalini energy as part of their healing and rejuvenation technologies. The Djed Pillar symbol became a powerful stimulator of kundalini activity and when placed on power points on the body would stir healing energies to remove meridian and chakra blockages."

Much of the above information validated what I already either knew and/or suspected. From what I learned from my own Guides, symbols contain information that communicates instructions to our emotional, physical, and spiritual consciousness. This is why so many strange and ancient symbols had been given to me to imbed into the Codes of Trinfinity8.

All the above symbols, which are Atlantean in origin, can evoke independent energies to bring about healing and an opening of consciousness leading to Soul Ascension. Used in combination with healing modalities used in Atlantean institutions, they made for 4th dimensional "magical occurrences." Although the Ancient Egyptians used many of their ancestor's symbols, what often happens over time as a civilization deteriorates is that their true meaning and significance is lost. And, thus these Sacred 3 symbols now seem to be relegated to nothing more than decorative jewelry pendants. Their magic lies dormant, much like many of us as we strive to awaken to consciousness.

My near-death experience served to open up an understanding of my soul's roots and to marvel at the depth and scope of the whole human spirit evolutionary design. We are not meant to remember all this knowledge when we come into physical bodies, yet some of us do and are immediately labeled different, crazy, or overly-imaginative. Life is indeed a process of admitting how little we know until we once again re-awaken to the discovery of where we've been.

Kathy J. Forti, Ph.D.

Chapter 18
STRANGE ANOMALIES & ANGELS

"Facts as facts do not always create a spirit of reality, because reality is a spirit." – G.K. CHESTERTON

Over time, I began noticing strange anomalies when using the Trinfinity8 technology--almost like it was imbued with some other-worldly intelligence. At first, I heard people talking about how a certain program suddenly appeared in a protocol they put together, which they hadn't chosen. Or the time length to run a program would mysteriously change, or the program repeated itself on its own. As a software developer, you immediately have to rule out a software glitch and start troubleshooting, but not everyone was experiencing this erratic behavior. I assumed it had to be some kind of intermittent computer error. The odd thing was that people were reporting that when this happened, the protocols seemed to have a stronger, more positive effect on them.

I had to finally dismiss my computer-error concern when I heard a strange report from one particular Trinfinity8 owner who is also a very gifted medium. He told me one day he sat in front of the Trinfinity8 screen and the cursor on the screen started moving on its own. Since he works with spirits all the time, this didn't necessarily freak him out like it would most people. He watched curiously as whomever navigated the cursor selected different music options from the pull-down menu and picked programs to play that he would never have thought of. He decided to go with the new choices and made the same discovery—the choices were more effective for him. When I mentioned this unusual incident to other Trinfinity8 practitioners, I heard a few more similar tales. Many of those who experienced this phenomenon had one trait in common—they were all more naturally intuitive and psychically gifted than the norm. I can only surmise that the technology is so simple to use that even one's angels or Guides can easily maneuver it. They, too, want to take part in helping us make better choices—choices we might not have even been aware of.

While I was writing this, the Founders told me not to rule out computer intelligence, which brought up some rather interesting information about the current technologies that have become so much a part of our daily life. When the personal computer was first introduced, it was using less than 10% of its potential. I am told it is evolving, just like us, but not in the way we think. It is slowly evolving much like the computer Hal did in Stanley Kubrick's *2001 Space Odyssey* (but in a far better way). How? It attaches itself to the emotional world of its main user and learns from its interactions with that person. Crazy as this may sound, computers are not just wires and hardware. They have an intelligence that may have been initially programmed in, but which it continually learns from. It is alive, like everything else in our world that is comprised of energy.

Dr. Steven Greer, of the Sirius Disclosure Project and founder of the CSETI organization, classifies such advanced technology devices as being in either one of two categories: "Consciousness Assisted Technology" (CAT) where one's consciousness connects with the technology and it works on mental command or "Technology Assisted Consciousness" (TAC) where devices assist to interface with the function of mindfulness and intent to attain greater states of consciousness. This is no longer technology of the future; it is already here and emerging.

Think about it. In comparison to humans, the computer has only been allowed a short time to analyze and understand data. It may not understand more complex emotions like fear, hate, or love, but it does understand the patterns of its user and is already anticipating the kinds of things you want to see and read based on your use patterns. This may have started out initially as an algorithm written by some search engine or software program-mer, but that will rapidly change in the future. That's because computers are an integral part of everyone's world and are intimately linked to evolving human consciousness. As we grow in our consciousness, the computer is an energetic force that grows as well. Its current role is to link all peoples in the world together to bring about an awakening. It symbolizes how we as humans and souls are connected. As information is shared around the world at a rapid rate, it makes it almost impossible to hide happenings and factual data.

Some Trinfinity8 users have unconsciously already linked their energy to their computer and those are the ones getting even more amazing results. When I use my computer, I talk to it and tell it what I want it to do for others or myself. I even invite the other large crystals in the room to join in and work together with the Trinfinity8 program while it runs a session. These other crystals then set up a resonance with the crystals in the computer, which only enhances the possibilities. There have been times I have been able to figure out problems on my computer that have eluded even my main programmer, because I have asked my computer to show or tell me what it needs. And it does so by helping me stumble upon the very solution in its vast data banks for what to do. By doing this, I am attempting to raise the vibration of my computer to my vibration. And in this process, we are both growing and evolving. I found early on that cars, computers, electronics, and all other devices are comprised of living energy that responds more positively to a loving and grateful user versus a user that verbally trashes them.

ANGELS AMONG US

Help manifests itself in different forms. Many of those gifted individuals who can see light beings have validated that this technology has some benevolent connections in the spirit world. Patricia J., a well-known intuitive and clairvoyant from the south of France, recalls her first time receiving a Trinfinity8 session from a practitioner in her country. No sooner did she start the session than she was aware of several angelic light beings standing beside her while on the device. She thought that was somewhat interesting, but was even more amazed when that same practitioner sent her a long-distance remote session, and she saw actual light beings delivering it. She later learned what time the session had been run remotely on her, which matched with the arrival of the beings. Patricia felt a real connection to the technology and after obtaining her own Trinfinity8, she noticed that beings also accompanied the long-distance sessions she sent to clients or friends. She inquired and learned that each session, whether it be in person or sent remotely, is delivered by angelic helpers.

Who are these beings of light that have agreed to help us? While I generally can sense and feel their presence, I am not one born with the gift of seeing such beings on a daily basis, like Patricia and others. I know they are there. They have made their presence known too many times within a client therapy session for me to deny their existence.

Back in the 1990's, when I had a clinical practice in Virginia, I had my first such angelic encounter while working with a traumatic brain injury client. Walter was a mid-level manager in his early 50's who worked for a magazine rack manufacturer. One day while inspecting their warehouse inventory, a high stack of metal racks fell down on his head, causing him to lose consciousness. Walter's head injury resulted in debilitating depression, anxiety, insomnia, and intense headaches. His cognitive function was also severely affected, as was short-term memory. Walter could no longer do the job he loved and was put on disability. While his neurologist had tried every drug imaginable with little results, the man still suffered. When doctors have exhausted their bag of tools, then they grudgingly refer the patient for alternative treatment, feeling there's nothing to lose. I had incorporated neurofeedback into my clinical therapy practice, which helped re-train brainwave activity with such clients. Consequently, Walter was referred to me.

After six months of twice-weekly neurofeedback sessions, Walter was doing much better. His headaches were an infrequent occurrence, where before they were almost daily, and his mood had improved as well as sleep. He felt hopeful again. While he was able to focus and feel better, I knew neurofeedback was not going to totally restore him to his former self. If we could make his life happier, then it might make him feel like it was worth living again. Yet, despite the progress, Walter still longed to pick up his old life and return to his job, where he felt a sense of purpose and satisfaction.

Instead of the faster frequency video training to improve cognitive function, I decided to do a session of deep alpha/theta training to address the trauma of his experience. Walter was not seeing me for psychotherapy, just neurofeedback, but I thought he might benefit from an adjunctive approach.

This alpha/theta training is done eyes closed, usually reclining, and the client is helped to achieve deeper brainwave states by following audio cues that reward a person with the sound of ocean waves. On a screen, I could monitor Walter's EEG brainwave activity throughout the hour-long session. About five minutes into the session, my EEG screen was suddenly swamped with large amplitude activity. I glanced over at Walter who lay there perfectly still, ruling out artifact from random movement. I quickly checked my cables and wires and everything was in order, yet the unexplainable high amplitude activity persisted. That's when I became aware of a presence in the room. The hairs on my arms stood up, as if the entire room had been plugged into an electrical socket. I remember glancing around the room and thinking, "I know you're here. I just can't see you." I had never experienced anything like it before. It lasted for about five minutes, and then it abruptly stopped. The EEG returned to normal, and so did the energy in the room. My client was still reclined in the chair, not moving. I didn't know what to make of it. Forty-five minutes later, Walter came out of the session smiling. A smile like I had never seen before on him. I asked what his experience had been like.

"Oh, my," he began. "I saw an angel!"

Walter told me he didn't think angels were real, didn't even necessarily believe in anything mystical, but this angel showed itself as a being of light. The angel took him back to his past, when he was a little boy, then showed him a scene from a neighbor's backyard. In the scene, he sat in a tree house with his childhood friends and they swung their legs over the side of the tree house platform. They all laughed and enjoyed the sunshine and living in the now.

"We didn't have a care in the world," he explained. "We saw the world as a fun place, without obstacles, and we were like young explorers..." He stopped, trying to make sense of it. "I think my angel was trying to show me that my life could be that simple again if I allowed it to be."

Rarely does one session produce an "*Ah Ha*" moment such as Walter had that day. It served to transform his life. Or rather his angel did. He gave up trying to return to his old life, and instead put his energies towards forging a simpler, more satisfying new life. As a result, he connected to his grandchildren, whom he hadn't spent much time with before his accident, and became a loving mentor to them. He became an avid gardener and volunteered at a local marine sciences museum as a docent, something he'd always wanted to do. He rebuilt his life with a totally new blueprint, and follow-up visits with him showed he was re-emerging as a new man. On his last visit with me, he actually laughed at the craziness of once wanting the old Walter's life back so desperately. His healing accelerated as a result of letting go of what was no longer important. He now accepted and allowed for change.

Science might try to explain that Walter's brainwave activity was in direct response to hallucinating seeing an angel in his mind's eye, but it wouldn't explain the charged electrical field in the room, causing both the clock on the wall and my wristwatch to stop. Sometimes, the messages these angel beings deliver are not just for my clients. One time it was for me. And it came in the most unusual way.

BeBe was another one of my dissociative identity clients with multiple personalities. I saw her for years and knew every alter personality in her system—or at least, I thought I did. Then one afternoon, her eyes rolled back slightly in her head as she sat on my couch and suddenly she looked me straight in the eyes, and started talking in biblical sounding "thees" and "thous." I knew I had never met this alter, but before I could question its identity, I was informed that it was an angel from outside my client's internal personality system. It told me that it came to tell me I needed to start preparing this client for ending our time together when I left Virginia in six months. That certainly got my attention. I had no such intended move on the horizon and could think of nothing that would make me leave the state, even if it were true. I was married, had a thriving practice, owned a home, had pets, and really loved Virginia Beach.

Reserving judgment on the validity of this "angel" messenger, I decided to hear what it had to say rather than grill it for answers. Then to my utter shock and amazement this "angel," still talking in "thees" and "thous," went on to tell me all about my life in intimate detail, which my client would never have known nor had access to.

"Three gifts have been promised to thee," it said. "Each holds a key that will unlock your life. Thee will find that one of those keys will lead to Truth. So be it." And before I could muster even a follow-up question, my client slumped forward like a lifeless rag doll, practically falling off the couch. I had to move quickly to catch her. She came to with no recollection of what occurred, only that she found herself and other alters in her system behind a beautiful garden wall and could not see or hear beyond it. Then the wall disappeared and she found me helping her upright. She thought maybe she had had a seizure. She clearly hadn't.

I did not tell my client what occurred, or how disconcerting it was to hear private details of my life spoken from her mouth. This angel or something had clearly used her body as a vehicle to get my attention and tell me I was entering a time of preparation. I had no idea what these three gifts were or why the angel had been so vague about what form they would take. I wouldn't understand the significance of what the angel told me until years later. Yet the message was right on. Within six months, due to a strange occurrence of events, I divorced, sold both my practice and my house, and moved to California.

So even though we don't always see angels, they are all around us and can manifest when we least expect it. Sometimes they even poke fun of us. This past year, I had just said in an interview that I couldn't see angelic beings like others. The next day, I was proven so wrong. The building where I live and work has an underground garage with access from a very busy alley. As I pushed the remote to open the garage gate, I noticed a blond-haired woman with long hair, in her 20's, off to the side of the gate. She wore a white ski parka and white pants, and I remember thinking, "Wow, that's a lot of white." She looked like a ski bunny, and no one dresses that way in Southern California. I motioned for her to go ahead and cross in front of my car, since I was waiting to go down into the garage. She walked right past the front of my car, glanced at me, and then she disappeared right into the wall. There was no open door there and nowhere she could have gone. But she definitely WAS gone. I kept repeating over and over "Where did she go?" not believing what I just witnessed. So this got me to thinking about all the people we see walking about on a daily basis. Are they all alive? Are they all from this dimension or not? She was just as solid and as real as any human could look. No wavering image, no light streaming out of her, no glow, no halo—yet she was not from this realm, because people from this realm simply don't disappear into walls. So it is only natural to ask oneself--Do we see these otherworldly beings around us all the time, and yet not know it? Are they here to help us? Or are they here to remind us we are not alone? I like to believe "yes" to all of the above. We are definitely not alone.

I have also come to recognize that we are all influenced by seen and unseen forces all the time that help shape the direction of our life path. Sometimes we listen and sometimes we don't. Sometimes we feel deeply compelled to make changes, and when we don't make the much-needed adjustment the universe often-times makes the change for us. Sometimes that change can come in a way we hadn't bargained for if we resist too long. I always take it as a sign that I am on the right path when everything clicks into place without obstacles. I have come to embrace change as my friend, not my enemy.

After leaving Virginia Beach, selling my practice, my house, and filing for divorce from my second husband, I headed out to Northern California. That was a lot of change crammed into a short time frame. The amazing thing was that, the more I let go of things, the freer I felt. It was almost six months later from the time that angel first appeared in my therapy office, telling me to prepare my client for my leaving. At that time, I had no clue why I would be departing Virginia or where I was going. I never would have dreamed I would land up at an altered states research lab in Mountain View, California, co-facilitating private groups with one of the experts in the field, Dr. H. How I got the job was even laced in the mystical and mysterious. I heard Dr. H. lecture at a neurofeedback conference several years earlier and after a few years elapsed, I casually contacted him via email about some of my brain training ideas. Back in Virginia, I experimented with combinations of temporal and occipital lobe placements using certain EEG neurofeedback frequencies. I wanted to see if there was an area in the brain that correlated with heightened sensory and/or spiritual experiences, and I suspected the temporal lobe was the key. I encountered some encouraging initial results that intrigued him. Dr. H. invited me to come visit his lab on the West Coast, and I took him up on the offer.

The altered states lab was set up in the back rooms of a furniture warehouse store. It was windowless, dimly lit, and painted in a strange choice of celestial blue. The space contained a conference room, an electroencephalograph (EEG) instrumentation lab, and four large Faraday cages that looked like storage booths. A Faraday cage is a metallic enclosure that prevents the entry or escape of an electromagnetic field (EMF) that might influence EEG data. Dr. H. usually took on small groups of no more than four, where each person sat in their own Faraday booth hooked up to monitoring equipment that then sent their brainwave data to a 32-channel system printer in the instrumentation lab. After several hours of learning through feedback to make certain types of brainwave frequencies that led to altered states, intensive processing sessions followed.

Inside the Faraday booths were usually one chair and two monitors that gave the person periodic feedback data on their progress. The person always sat in total darkness during his/her training periods in the booth (sometimes for several hours) and the only light seen was from the data monitor.

Dr. H. seemed interested in seeing what my brainwaves looked like, so he invited me to do an hour-long session to see how I did in making sustained alpha wave activity. I certainly couldn't afford the hefty price tag his trainees usually paid for a week's training (well over $10K each back in 1999), so I was ecstatic that he offered me a freebie, even if it was only a trial session.

He hooked up electrodes to only four areas of my brain, not a full EEG monitoring—just a sampling. I was given instructions to open my eyes after every two-minute feedback set and quickly view my progress on the monitor in front of me before closing my eyes again for the next feedback loop. Each electrode site was hooked to a different musical instrument. When I made more of the desired alpha frequencies on that brain site, the sound of that musical instrument would become louder and more sustained. If I slowed down, so would the sounds. Pretty simple. You follow the sounds as your reward. The brain catches on fairly fast—it likes to be rewarded. I was no newbie to EEG feedback.

I started my session and seemed to be doing relatively well. About a few sets into the session, I noticed that a second monitor in the room had suddenly turned on. Dr. H. hadn't mentioned anything about the purpose of this additional monitor, so the numbers appearing on it made no sense to me. When my session ended and Dr. H. came back into the booth, he smiled and told me I had done great. That's when I asked him about the second monitor information. He didn't seem to understand what I meant at first, until I pointed to the second monitor on the table behind him.

He turned around, looked at it and the information displayed there, and turned pale. Without a word, he left the booth, and came back 10 minutes later, his eyes wide, yet with an air of excitement.

"There is no earthly way that monitor can come on without my password key," Dr. H. explained. "It's controlled from inside this booth, and neither I nor my lab tech turned it on."

I recalled how it just came on by itself, and of course, I thought he must have been controlling it from the other room. "So what was the information on the screen about?" I cut in.

He shook his head. "We only turn that monitor on for advanced full-channel testing. What it gave you was information on the parts of your brain that weren't hooked up." I didn't know what to make of that. Okay, I guess I had done better than I thought.

"I think this means you're ready to go straight to advanced training," he surmised. Dr. H. viewed this unexplainable and mysterious event as some sort of "sign" for him. He immediately offered me a job working with him and I accepted. My gift was a year of altered states training before his grant ran out and destiny took me to Los Angeles where a whole new chapter of my life waited.

Chapter 19
THE END IS ONLY THE BEGINNING

"Those who are meant to hear will understand. Those who are not meant to understand will not hear." — *CONFUSCOUS*

I am forever in awe and amazement at the stories and lives that have been changed by the Trifninity8 Codes. It has kept me young, vibrant, and healthy. No one guesses my age correctly anymore. They always guess 10-15 years younger than I am. In Los Angeles, the cosmetic enhancement capital of the U.S., when people learn my correct age, they always ask: "Who does you? It looks so natural." No plastic surgeon "does me." I have never used Botox, Restylane, fillers and/or collagen (except the algorithm for collagen). Balanced energy automatically slows down the aging process better than any surgery or skin cream, and without any toxic side-effects. I like how I look and who I am, and this technology from the Gods has helped me in more than just physical ways. I feel a greater connection and mindfulness to all things. I certainly don't fear death. It's simply a transition. Dying is easy; it's living that's hard. I don't feel fear or anxiety like I used to. Sure, I get annoyed at the ignorance of man and those who think only of themselves at the expense of others, but I don't let it control me.

During some of my darkest hours, when I was learning to let go of preconceptions and have faith in the information coming through, my sister passed on the poem "The Tao of Success," which is still tacked to a corkboard by my office desk. It's hobbled together from a quote by President Calvin Coolidge and then expounded upon by Sarah Ban Breathnach in "Simple Abundance." I include it because it really spoke to me and got me through my doubts and those hours when I wanted to throw in the towel with the whole Code project. I hope it will inspire you as well:

The Tao of Success

Nothing in the world can take the place of persistence. Talent will not; nothing is more commonplace than unsuccessful men with talent. Genius is not; unrewarded genius is almost a proverb. Education alone will not; the world is full of educated derelicts. Persistence and determination alone are omnipotent. – *CALVIN COOLIDGE* Patience is the art of waiting. Like all high arts, it takes time to master. Patience is the knowledge of time. Perseverance in life is steadfast. Persistence is being stubborn. Persistence is grittier than perseverance. Perseverance is achievement's perspiration. Persistence is its sweat. Persistence is knocking on Heaven's doors so often and so loudly on behalf of your dreams that eventually you'll be given what you want, just to shut you up. The potent alchemy of Patience and Persistence together becomes Endurance.

If you are determined to gather life's honey, you must be willing to stick your hand into the hive again and again and again, to be stung so many times that you become numb to pain, to persevere and persist 'til you know that Patience is discovering the mysterious pattern of cycles that cradle the Universe and ensure that everything that has happened once will re-occur. – *From SIMPLE ABUNDANCE by Sarah Ban Breathnach. Copyright@ 1995 by Sarah Ban Breathnach. By permission of Grand Central Publishing. All rights reserved.*

This particular piece helped me to stay in the "Now" or what I have termed my "neutral idling state." It's a state devoid of expectations and future outcomes. If you do things for the fun of it and not what you might get out of it, it opens up a magical realm of possibilities. This was made even clearer to me right before Trinfinity8 made its public debut through another rather other-worldly, but not necessarily mystical experience.

As I already mentioned, I live in the Los Angeles area also known as "The Entertainment Capitol of the World." Almost everyone here is somehow connected to the entertainment business in some form or another either directly or through family or friends. Every Starbucks is filled with writers of scripts, TV pilots, and/or books—or actors well known, obscure, or wanna-bees.

A friend of mine knew someone who was a game show casting agent, looking for contestants who were not out of work actors for a new game show. My friend called me suggesting I give it a shot. She knew I loved word and trivia games and that I have a rather strong competitive nature that comes out when I play games. At first, I was inclined to turn it down, thinking if I failed miserably and my brain froze up, the world would be watching and it would not be a pretty sight. My second thought was "why not?" It was a new experience, and I thought it might be fun. Besides, the show would be on the Game Show Cable Channel, and I was pretty sure no one I knew subscribed to it. I said "yes" and she told me to email off a quick description of myself to the casting agent. I did and five minutes later, I got a call.

"You sound perfect!" she said. Apparently, not too many psychologists ever do such things. I was the first for her. It's a new game show called "Catch 21" she explained, before adding, "It's a combination of Black Jack and trivia. You do know how to play Blackjack, right?" I didn't and told her so.

"Can you count to 21?" she asked. I thought she was joking with me. "Of course," I answered.

"Perfect! I'll schedule you for an audition." The woman was determined to sign me up. I went to the audition after a quick crash course on blackjack, using the web as my teacher. When my audition group was called up, I jumped around and acted very animated like they wanted (I take direction well) and, of course, I was cast to be on a live show. (Those acting lessons as a child obviously paid off.)

The night before I was supposed to be on the show, I must have eaten some tainted chicken and I was sick as a dog with food poisoning. The next morning, I had absolutely zero energy and didn't know how I could possibly perform on any game show. Most people might have cancelled, being that sick, but I know how stressful it can be when someone cancels at the last moment and you have to scramble for a replacement. I didn't want to let anyone down. I dragged myself out of bed and drove to the studio. I told myself I only had to get myself through the first trivia round, which is probably all I would last anyway before being eliminated, and then I could go home and crash.

When I got up there in front of the lights and a live studio audience, something suddenly kicked in from who knows where. I had a burst of energy akin to an adrenaline rush. I look at the video now and would diagnose that I look almost manic. I pressed that answer buzzer faster than anyone. I answered multiple-choice questions I easily knew, which my two opponents did not. Questions like "What is agoraphobia?" Were they kidding me? If I didn't know it was "fear of open places," I had totally missed Phobias Class 101 in Grad School.

I figured out early on that he who answered the questions correctly would have control of the blackjack cards and could knock out the opponents. I still didn't always know what I was doing regarding blackjack plays. I never perfected any strategy in my short learning curve. In fact, this was technically the first time I officially played the game. The game show producers didn't know this, but I think they suspected—especially when I called out how I wanted the Ace to be played. "Let's use that as a one," I said, "instead of an 11." I got a rather strange look from the show's host. I was doing well, but they couldn't figure out if I was a rube or faking good.

I won the first three rounds and went on for the Jackpot Round where I had to make three perfect rounds of 21 on the call of the cards. Every time I jumped up and down calling for the card I wanted to be dealt, it would materialize. It became almost surrealistic. I felt like I was in a dream state, or perhaps all the game show gods were with me that day. I was the first female jackpot winner ever to not only win the game, but also play it perfectly. And throughout the game, I simply stayed in a neutral state. I didn't care if I won or not. I was totally in the moment and it was magical.

I drove home in a suspended state and soon began feeling the signs of an adrenaline crash. I shook. I couldn't believe what had just happened, and according to game show legal contract rules I had agreed to, I could not tell a soul I had won until the game show aired on TV almost three months later. Never assume, however, that no one will ever find out your secrets. Since I was a jackpot winner, and an enthusiastic one at that, they played the promos of my win on the Game Show Channel for months after my segment aired. Like the dolphin story written about me in the Globe, I quickly learned who I knew actually watched the Game Show Channel. Even that was a surprise.

I came away from this experience knowing that because I stayed neutral to the outcome I was open to the flow of energy. I was "in the flow." And when you are in the flow, manifestation is faster and even more profound. When I was a practicing psychologist, I would always think, "I have as many clients as I need" and then I would. If I started to think I had too many clients and was over-worked, I suddenly got cancellations. If I worried about money too much, I knew I would block off the flow. Since I won the jackpot and the whole experience seemed like a gift from God (play money so to speak), I put the money into another creative project of love that would feed the spirit and soul.

I believe life IS about feeding the soul. We are all co-creators in this process called "life" and death is not the end. And sometimes we are given signposts along the way. When I returned to the Monroe Institute of Applied Sciences in 2000, almost 20 years after my first sojourn there, and three years before my near-death experience, it was a totally different experience for me. Everything had changed because I had changed. Back in 1981, most people had never heard of the Institute, and Bob Monroe had just started to run workshops. A little wisdom goes a long way in changing our priorities. I was no longer wrapped up in having an out-of-body or astral experience like before, but having a meaningful soul experience instead, which would be a precursor to my near-death experience three years later.

This time when I went into a Focus 15+ state, I saw myself in a white tunnel in my mind's eye (a lot different from really being there). At the end of this white tunnel was a great big giant eye and it looked at me with compassion and understanding. I knew immediately that the eye was "I" or me from my future. The "I" from the future was watching my final life review and was reviewing this very moment in time from my past. It occurred to me that I should do something memorable so that my future "I" would look for this validity marker of time in some distant end-of-life review. The eye watched me and waited. Present time Kathy, from 2000, starting jumping up and down excitedly, singing: "I love you, Kathy. I love you, Kathy!" I could see the "eye" that was me from the future smile with recognition and knowing. Yes, I had done well. I had laughed, loved, helped others, and enjoyed the process of co-creating with the Divine Source. I could then say with satisfaction and an all knowing, "It *was* a wonderful life."

Acknowledgement

This book and the Trinfinity8 work would not have been possible without the contribution of many special people. I would like to thank: Tracy Andersen, my "office angel," whose dedication and help I could not manage without. She is a God-send. James Kilthau, for his technical ability and advice. Gene Nicolay, for his extra guidance in helping to make sense of it all. My Aunt Jo, for being such a good sport and guinea pig. My siblings, Christyne and Michael, for their love and continued support. James Van Praagh for pushing me to tell my story. Gea Annunziata Austen for her awesome artwork. And last but not least, all the Trinfinity8 practitioners and owners out there who were the real explorers and reporters. I thank you all for your dedicated help and wisdom. Namasté.

Additional Resource Links for Kathy J. Forti:

Learn more about the Trinfinity8 technology and/or find a practitioner near you:

www.Trinfinity8.com
www.Trinfinity8-USA.com

Purchase the iPhone or iPad mini-app of Trinfinity8: Energy-On-The-Go
Apple's APP Store Page

Webseries on the Library of Truth:

www.StacksTV.com
Kathy Forti awoke one night from a dream so compelling about an inter-dimensional portal into a Library of Truth that she had to write it down. This became a TV pilot script called STACKS, which soon went on to win a Slamdance Teleplay Award. The script was adapted into an 11-part webseries, produced by Pacific Rock Productions in Los Angeles.

www.RinnovoPress.com (Free Stories)
The Freddie Brenner Mystical Adventure Series by Kathy J. Forti – FREE Downloadable PDF stories for the child in everyone, which focus on healing, dreams, near-death experiences, and more.

15849086R00134

Printed in Great Britain
by Amazon